PORTRAITS
of
BIBLE MEN

Third Series

Titles in the "Portraits of Bible Characters" series:

PORTRAITS OF BIBLE MEN — First series
 Adam, Abel, Enoch, Noah, Abraham, Isaac,
 Jacob, Joseph, Moses, Joshua, Samuel, David,
 Solomon, Elijah, Elisha, Job

PORTRAITS OF BIBLE MEN — Second series
 Ishmael, Lot, Melchisedek, Balaam, Aaron,
 Caleb, Boaz, Gideon, Jonathan,
 Mephibosheth, Jonah, Hezekiah, Isaiah,
 Jeremiah, Ezekiel, Daniel

PORTRAITS OF BIBLE MEN — Third series
 John the Baptist, John, Nathanael, Peter,
 Nicodemus, Thomas, Philip, Matthew,
 Zacchaeus, James, Barnabas, Mark, Cornelius,
 Timothy, Paul

PORTRAITS OF BIBLE WOMEN
 Eve, Sarah, Rebekah, Rachel, Miriam,
 Deborah, Ruth, Hannah, Mary, the mother of
 Christ, Mary, Mary Magdalene

George Matheson

PORTRAITS
of
BIBLE MEN

Third Series

**Foreword by
Warren W. Wiersbe**

K

KREGEL PUBLICATIONS
Grand Rapids, Michigan 49501

Portraits of Bible Men (Third Series) by George Matheson.
Copyright © 1987 by Kregel Publications, a division of Kregel,
Inc. All rights reserved.

Library of Congress Cataloging-in-Publication Data

Matheson, George, 1842-1906.
    Portraits of Bible Men. Third Series.

    Reprint. Originally published: Representative Men of the
New Testament. 2nd ed. London: Hodder and Stoughton,
1910.
    1. Bible. N.T.—Biography, I. Title.
BS2430.M3   1987   225.9'22 [B]   86-27220
ISBN 0-8254-3253-7

1 2 3 4 5 Printing/Year 91 90 89 88 87

Printed in the United States of America.

Contents

Foreword

GEORGE Matheson was blind, but with the "eyes of his heart" he could see farther and deeper than most of us. This was especially true when it came to penetrating the minds and hearts of the great Bible characters. In my opinion, no evangelical writer, including the great Alexander Whyte, surpasses George Matheson in this whole area of Bible biography. The Bible teacher or preacher who wants to grasp the significance of these important Bible characters should read Matheson and give serious consideration to his insights.

Matheson was born in Glasgow, Scotland, March 27, 1842. Early in his life, his eyesight began to fail; but he managed to complete his basic schooling with the aid of strong glasses.

From that time on, he had to have assistance with his studies; and his two sisters nobly stood by him. He earned two degrees at the University of Glasgow, felt a call to the ministry, and was licensed by the Glasgow Presbytery on June 13, 1866. He became assistant to J. R. McDuff, the well-known devotional writer, and then accepted the pastorate of the church of Innellan. He was ordained on April 8, 1868.

Like many young preachers at that time, Matheson experienced a personal "eclipse of faith" and even considered abandoning the ministry. His church officers were understanding and compassionate and advised him to stay on and give God an opportunity to deepen his faith. In due time, the young minister came out of the furnace with stronger faith and a deeper understanding of God's eternal message.

It seems incredible that a blind minister in that day could accomplish all that George Matheson accomplished. He became an outstanding scholar and theologian, as well as a gifted devotional writer and preacher. Others, of course, read to him; but it was he who assembled the materials and prepared each message. He *memorized* his sermon, the Scripture lessons and the hymns; and it was said that he never missed a word! He was diligent to visit his people and enter into their joys and trials. In every way, George Matheson was a devoted pastor and preacher.

It is unfortunate that Matheson is remembered today primarily as the author of the hymn, "O Love That Wilt Not Let Me Go," because his books of devotional essays and his biographical studies are rich mines of spiritual truth for the serious Bible student. In my own sermon preparation and writing ministry, I have often turned to Matheson to discover penetrating insights into familiar verses and exciting lessons from the lives of familiar Bible characters. What George Matheson has written may not move you, but it certainly excites me!

After hearing George Matheson preach, a Scottish Presbyterian Council publicly declared: "The Council all feel that God has closed your eyes only to open other eyes, which have made you one of the guides of men." I trust that you will come to the same conclusion as you read these chapters.

WARREN W. WIERSBE

Back to the Bible,
Lincoln, Nebraska

1

Introduction

THERE are moments in the history of this world which may be called moments of ingathering. Their mission is to collect the experiences of the past and bind them into unity. The most striking of all such moments is the advent of Christ. To the men who witnessed that advent it presented an appearance which they have described by one word, ' fulness.' In the heart of the Roman Empire there stood forth a man who resembled in His nature nothing so much as that empire itself. Rome was not a country of the earth; she was a country that had become the earth. She had gathered into her bosom the once separate lands and bound them by a silver chain; she represented to the view of the spectator not a nation, but the human race.

So was it with the man Christ Jesus. He was a mirror of that empire into which He was born. If Rome united in her constitution all dominions and powers, Jesus united in His person all types of character. The rivers of every land had run into this human sea. The earnestness of Judah was there; the buoyancy of Greece was there; the mysticism of India was there; the practicalness of China was there; the legal acumen of Rome herself was there. There dwelt the self-restraint of the Stoic, the easy mind of the Epicurean, the winged imagination of the Platonist. There reposed side by side things which naturally fly apart—the simplicity of Galilee and the subtlety of Jerusalem, the gravity of the East and the sparkle of the West, the devotion of the Brahman to the soul, and that care for the wants of the body which constitutes the essence of the European life.

If you wish to see the fulness of the life of Christ just put to yourself one question. Retracing the steps through that Gallery of the Old Testament which we have traversed, and taking at random any great quality expressed by any figure, simply ask yourself, Is not this equally represented in the life of Jesus ? Has Enoch a vision of immortality ; Christ professes to reveal life eternal. Is Noah a preacher of righteousness ; Christ calls sinners to repentance. Has Abraham a dream of universal empire ; Christ claims to found a kingdom of God. Does Isaac represent home-life ; so does Christ at Bethany. Does Jacob aspire to a priesthood ; Christ offers Himself for a world's sin. Is Moses the law-giver on Sinai ; Christ is the law-giver on Hermon. Is David chivalrous to his foes ; Christ forgives His enemies. I do not know a phase of Old Testament heroism which has not been reproduced in the Picture of Jesus. The calm wisdom of Solomon is here, side by side with the flashing of Elijah's fire. The fine courtesy of Boaz is here, hand in hand with Elisha's denunciation of wrong. The daring fearlessness of Daniel is here, blended in equal measure with Job's patient endurance. The humanitarian sweep of Isaiah is here, but along with it there is something which such universal sympathy is apt to exclude—the capacity for individual friendship which marks the soul of Jonathan.

It seems to me that such a mode of experimenting on the Sacred Gallery would be a real test of 'the fulness of Him that filleth all in all.' One who was almost a contemporary of the Galilean ministry speaks of Christ as destined in the future to gather all things to Himself. But, from an artistic point of view, this gathering was already completed. The Portrait of Jesus is not the representative of a phase of humanity; it is humanity itself. He unites in one face and form the faces and forms of the whole past Gallery. He represents no special quality; He expresses all qualities and He expresses all specially—in a pronounced degree. It is written, 'When the fulness of the time was come God sent His Son.' The fulness of the time was the time for fulness. It was the age when the rivers were to be ripe for being gathered into the sea, when the planets were to be ready for incorporation in the solar beam. The human side of Christianity was to be not the revelation of a man, but the revelation of Man. I read in the Book of Genesis that 'in the beginning God created the heavens and the earth'—that the first thing on which He gazed was not a part but the whole. So has it been with the genesis of Christianity. The first thing which appeared to the eye of the spectator was its entire heaven and its entire earth. Future years would exhibit the separate items—sun, moon, and star—herb, plant, and tree. But the *morning* of Christianity was the union of all things. All gifts and graces were embraced in a single life—the man Christ Jesus. The colours of that life, which one day were to be distributed among different flowers, were beheld at first concentrated in a rainbow. The garment which to-morrow was to be parted among many bore to-day the aspect of a single robe whose richness enwrapped one human spirit, and whose folds were covering one individual form.

In the primitive stage of village life we

commonly find all commodities embraced in a single store. People go there for the most unlike things—daily food, medicine, millinery, house-letting, carriage-driving, registration, banking, the offices of the smith and the carpenter—perhaps even of the lawyer and the preacher. The time will come when each of these will form its separate craft. But in the primitive village they are apt to be vested in a single life—a life of which we might say, in adaptation of the words of Scripture, 'of its fulness have we all received.' Now, this is precisely the case of primitive Christianity. All its varied glories which one day are to be disseminated are heaped up in a single soul. Like the nebular fire-cloud, it holds the fulness of all things. There sleeps the summary of the past ; there lies the germ of the future. Experiences the most diverse are there. The uncanonical Melchisedek and the priestly Aaron, the strong Ishmael and the tender Abel, the optimistic Joseph and the sad Jeremiah, the child Samuel and the manly Joshua, the expectant Caleb and the retro-

spective Hezekiah, the dependent Mephibosheth and the all-conquering Gideon—they
each rest there. It would seem as if the river
of Paradise had for a moment gathered back
into her bosom those streams from which she
had parted, and revealed within the compass
of one garden the manifold grace of God.
Christianity began where all life begins—in a
single cell—enfolding within the walls of a
seemingly insignificant dwelling the nucleus of
a new heaven and a new earth.

And now I come to a crucial question. I
hear the reader say : ' If this Portrait of Jesus
has gathered up the past, and if the future is
to be simply a repetition of its glories, why do
you speak of new *representative* men ! Nay,
on such a principle, why should you even
speak of a New Testament ! What is new
about it ! You have shown in the Old Gallery
every conceivable quality depicted that can
belong to a human soul. You show at the
opening of the Christian dispensation these
qualities united in a single life. You tell us
that in the coming section of the Gallery the

qualities thus united are again to be distributed in separate individual portraits. In
such a process where is there any room for
novelty! Is it not simply a repetition of old
qualities! Do we not get out of the box
exactly what we put in! Has the Old Testament Gallery left any phase of mind without
a record! How shall we distinguish between
the fire of an Elijah and the fire of a Peter!
How shall we discriminate between the un-
selfishness of an Abraham and the unselfish-
ness of a Paul! How shall we draw the line
between the friendship of a Jonathan and the
friendship of a John!' These are crucial
questions, and they are pertinent questions.
They await every man who attempts to deal
with the representative men of the Bible.
If Christ is at once the flower of the past
and the bud of the future, then the qualities
of the future must be simply the qualities of
the past. And if it be so, is not our progress merely a circle, our development only
a dream! It seems a misnomer to speak of
'the new man'—to say that if a man is in

Christ he is 'a new creature.' Where is the
novelty if I have simply climbed the wall
to see the fields of childhood! Would it not
be more correct to reverse the words of Paul
and say, 'To be in Christ is to retrace our
yesterday; new things have passed away and
all things have become old'!

But let us look deeper and this impression
itself will pass away. What is the account
which the New Testament Gallery gives of its
own development?—by that it ought to be
judged, by that it should stand or fall. Now,
it so happens that a spectator of this gallery
has given us a very clear view of what in his
opinion its figures were meant to represent.
He says, 'It was worthy of Him of whom are
all things and to whom are all things, in
bringing many sons unto glory, to make the
captain of their salvation perfect through
sufferings.' Here, by the glance of one
piercing eye, is the nature of the New Gallery
revealed! It is not a new assemblage of
qualities; it is a new mode of acquiring them.
In the old dispensation these qualities were

the gifts of Nature. Men were born with them; they were the native soil of the heart. They came to each soul as naturally as air comes, as food comes, as pastime comes. But in the new dispensation—in the section of the Gallery which was about to open, there was to be a change of ground. The qualities which had been native to the soul were to become the fruit of struggle. Men were no longer to be born with them; they were to win them—to attain them through conflict, to reach them by suffering. The difference between the Old Gallery and the New is the difference between temperament and grace; temperament is a planting, grace is a supplanting. Joseph is an optimist and Peter is an optimist; but the optimism of Joseph is very different from the optimism of Peter. Joseph was hopeful from disposition — he found the flowers in his cradle and he treasured them in his heart; Peter was hopeful as the result of experience—he began life amid the briars and he *transformed* them into flowers. This is a typical instance. It expresses in a single sentence my whole view of the difference between the New Gallery and the Old. In coming to Christ we are coming to the winepress. We are approaching a transforming process. We are entering upon a stage in which character is to be built, not born. We are coming to a period in which the wild flower is to give place to the flower of cultivation, and where a kingdom which belonged to hereditary transmission is to be won by the power of the sword.

Here, then, is the nature of the New Evangel —perfection through suffering—the attainment of a quality as the result of struggle. It would not in the least minimise the difference between the two Galleries if you could prove that the gentleness of Ruth was as perfect as the gentleness of John. The gentleness of Ruth originates in a different source from the gentleness of John. The former was a birthright; the latter was a conquest. The former was a gift of nature; the latter was a trophy of grace. The former was a spontaneous breath of the morning; the latter was a delicious fragrance which had been gathered in the afternoon. Christianity is perfection through suffering, excellence through suffering. Even where its fruits are less beautiful than the fruits of Judaism, they are more precious; they can stand the storm. Judaism shrank from the storm; its virtues tended to wither before the blast. But the virtues of Christianity were to be *brought* upon the blast. They were to come to the soul on the wings of the wind. They were to be the product not of spring but of autumn, not of hereditary bias but of stern experience. Christian faith demanded a cloud. Christian courage demanded a fear. Christian love demanded an impediment. Christian peace demanded a struggle. Christian purity demanded a meeting with the tempter in the wilderness.

Now, in the light of this contrast, I shall look at the New Testament Gallery from a different standpoint to that from which I surveyed the Old. In the previous volumes each portrait was accompanied by an adjective expressing its quality. I shall now assign to each portrait, not a descriptive adjective, but a descriptive verb—a verb indicating the particular influence which has been exerted over the man and which has transformed the man. I should say that in this world there are always the two classes—the men represented by the adjective, and the men represented by the verb; the one are the sons of nature, the other the sons of grace. The Old Gallery represents the first; upon the face of its portraits is stamped the impress of a quality. But the New Gallery opens another sphere. Here the faces of the men reveal, not the quality, but the action. The stamp which distinguishes these is not so much a possession as a struggle. We behold some of them advancing to the battle, some in the heat of the fight, some returning from victory; but all equally give the impression of a life being moulded by conflict. The watchword of this gallery is, 'Ye must become as little children.' The stress lies not on the word 'children' but on the word 'become.'

Childhood is a natural possession of all men, and its flowers may grow in every field. But if childhood be lost and won again, it is no longer a mere gift of nature; it is a triumph of grace. It is a pearl of great price from the simple fact that a price is paid for it, a sacrifice made for it. To be a guileless man under the fig-tree may be beautiful, but it is the beauty of a star; to be guileless amid the haunts of Nazareth, is the indication of a higher force of character—it is the beauty of a soul.

It may seem a strange thing that the struggle should have come in an age of peace. The dawn of Christianity was on a summer morning. It came when the political sky was clear. The songs of Bethlehem that proclaimed goodwill among men had already in a measure been realised. The earlier ages had been times of turbulence; the immediately succeeding ages were to be times of turbulence again. But this was a calm between two whirlwinds—short-lived, but very real. Men for an hour had beat their swords into ploughshares and their spears into pruning-hooks, and it seemed to many as if they would learn the art of war no more. Such was the age into which Christ was born. Is it not a singular thing that this, of all times, should have been the day of moral struggle—the day when the flowers of the heart did not spring spontaneously! We should have expected that the years of *war* would have been the years of moral crisis—that the hours of danger and terror and sword would have been the hours in which the inward lives of men would have undergone their vital change.

Yet, in this expectation, I think we are guided by an erroneous idea. Is it the case that the times of outward war are the times of inward conflict? I do not think so. To my mind, the struggles of the soul have always been deepest in the ages of peace. The times of war leave no leisure for looking within. They bring forth brilliant qualities, but they bring them forth without tillage, and they maintain them without the consciousness of their possessor. The times of physical danger are like the mists in the Book of Genesis which were sent up to water the ground. They indeed water the ground, but they are apt to hide the process of their own working. Before a man can look into himself, you must clear away the outward mist. Danger is unfavourable to introspection; even a boy at school will forget his answer if you hold the rod over him. The truth must be spoken: Peace, and not war, is the vivifier of this world. I used to think it an anticlimax when I read the prophet's longing for the day when the soldier should become a ploughman; but that was because I thought the age of the soldier was the age of deeper evolution. I know better now. The real struggle of life begins when the mind is at leisure from its surroundings. It is when a man rests from his outward troubles that he begins to strive with himself. Christ said that He came not to send peace, but a sword. Yes; and He sent the inward sword just because it was a time of outward peace. Had Cæsar been at war with the *world* Christ could never have waged war in the soul. The war in the soul demands a summer day—a day in which we are not molested from without. Christ tells His followers to pray that their flight be not in the winter, and He says well. Winter drives back into the old path and arrests the upward tendency. The misfortunes of life require all our energies for themselves; to turn these energies inward we need a voice upon the outward sea, 'Peace, be still!'

But there is a second characteristic of this coming Christian age which is well worthy of attention. Not only is it to be a period of *inward* transformation but of rapid transformation. This quality of the Messianic age had been anticipated by far-seeing minds. I do not think we attach the real meaning to the prophetic words of the later Isaiah, 'I the Lord will hasten it in its time.' We commonly understand the saying to mean that the time intervening till the Messiah comes will be short. To my mind, that is not what the Prophet desires to say. I understand him to proclaim his conviction that after the Messiah *has* come things will move at a double-quick march. The idea is, not that the coming of the kingdom will be accelerated, but that, when the kingdom has actually arisen, there will be times of acceleration. It is equivalent to saying, 'In the days of the Messiah God will cause all things to travel at a rapid pace.' Now, we all know that there are times of acceleration in the history of this world—times in which, to use a Bible phrase, a nation is born in a day. Events to which we looked forward as involving the march of centuries are seen to spring up in a night. Developments of character whose completion we predicted for the end of years are effected by the heat of a single summer. Lives which we thought would require a series of incarnations to perfect them are made to flower out by one drastic experience, and the work which naturally would have belonged to days is finished and culminated by the pressure of an hour.

Now, the advent of Christ is one of these times. It is a season of accelerated movements. The men of the Old Testament grow;

the men of the New flash. For, what is the
spectacle which the Christian Gallery reveals?
It is a series of figures rapidly discarding their
original costume and appearing in a garb of
contrary mould. We catch the momentary
glimpse of a fiery persecutor—it is Saul of
Tarsus; we turn aside for an instant, and,
when next we look, we are in the presence
of a son of charity. We see a man flying
from the post of duty because it is the post
of danger—it is Simon Peter; we avert our
eyes in disgust. The next moment the man
stands before us in an opposite vesture:
instead of shunning duty through fear of
danger, he is almost making danger itself a
duty. We behold a rather narrow Churchman,
devoted to externals and eager for ecclesiastical power—it is John, son of Zebedee. We
divert our gaze for a moment toward other
things. By and by we look again, and lo,
the man has lost his formalism, lost his
ecclesiasticism, lost his pride, and is found
reclining on the bosom of love!

How shall we account for this? Shall

we say that it is magical? No; there has not been one step omitted from the process of normal development. What has happened is that the development has been quickened. The stages of the process have not been abridged, but they have been hurried on. The kindling of the flower has been accelerated by the influence of a special atmosphere. What is that atmosphere? What should we expect it to be? Do we know of any influence which has a special power of accelerating? Yes—the contact with a great personality. I do not know of anything in the world which has such power to hasten the steps of the mind. A man may live for a whole lifetime amid the loveliest and grandest scenery the eye can dwell on, and he may remain at the end as stolid, as dull, as lethargic as when first he saw the light. But let that man meet with another man — a higher man, a man of piercing brain and potent heart and mesmeric attraction—you will see in a week an absolutely radical change. The eye will glisten, the step will lighten, the face will brighten; it will be like the dawning of an inward day. Nature has lofty thoughts for those who are already lofty, but she cannot speak *down* — cannot address her message to a dormant mind. This is precisely what a high soul *can* do. The higher it is, the easier for that soul to speak down. The deepest student of a subject will best educate the novice, and will most quickly educate the novice. There is no influence so accelerating as a human influence; one day in its courts is better than a thousand days in the courts of visible nature.

And the men of Galilee had come under a human influence. They had long been under the influence of inspiring scenery, that is to say, of scenery which would have inspired cultivated minds; yet it had failed to move them from their rustic apathy. But suddenly a *man* appeared! In the midst of the field there stood forth an extraordinary presence! We may call him by what name we will — teacher, preacher, reformer, philanthropist;

his immediate influence was something distinct from any of these. It was not what he taught, not what he preached, not what he amended; it was his creation of the sense of wonder. Human intelligence begins not with an act of understanding, but with the feeling that there is something which is not understood. The first step in every upward development is the sense of wonder; until that has come, we are dormant. The earliest power of Jesus was His waking the men of Galilee to wonder. He did for these men what the hills could not do, what the woods could not do, what the stars could not do; He made them ask questions. It is the question, not the answer, that is the note of dawn. My milestones lie in my mysteries—not in my acquirements. Galilee struck a new hour when it cried, 'What manner of man is this!' It knocked at its first gate of wonder. It learned for the first time that there was something it could see and not perceive, something it could hear and not understand. That sense of ignorance was worth all the knowledge in the world. It was the first leap out of the darkness, the earliest emergence into light. The dove had begun to move on the face of the waters, and its very unrest suggested the promise of a new land.

SON of Man, Thou hast the key to the Second Gallery — nay, Thou *art* the key! In Thee alone I learn the secret of the world's unrest. Thou Thyself art the secret. We speak of the waters being stilled by Thy coming; nay, it was Thy coming that *stirred* the waters. The faces of the New Gallery through which I am to pass are all the faces of struggling men; but their struggle comes from light, not darkness; they have seen *Thee*! They have lost their primitive satisfaction. There is a far look-out in the eyes, as if they sought something not here, as if they heard the murmuring of a distant sea. It is because they have seen *Thee*! Thy glory has left a cloud upon the common day. The lily of the field is less fair. The song of the bird is less buoyant. The scent of the hay is less sweet. The blue of the sky is less pure. The bosom of the sea is less calm. It is all from sight of *Thee*! Thy sheen has thrown all things into shade. Thy radiance has broken their rest. Thy beauty has tarnished their beam. Thy sweetness has blunted their savour. They have faded in front of Thy flower; they have vanished in touch of Thy voice; they have paled in the power of Thy presence; they have melted in the blaze of Thy music. The men of this New Gallery are less content with wood and field; but it is because their eyes have gazed on a higher loveliness—the brightness of Thy face!

2

John the Expanded

ON the threshold of the New Gallery we are
met by a portentous figure popularly known
as John the Baptist. He was the earliest
product of the influence of that Great Light
which was about to transform the world. In
order of time he is the first Christian. He
discerned the greatness of Jesus when, outwardly, Jesus was not great. He was the
earliest who fixed his eyes upon the miracle
of Christ's *character*. Nay, I am disposed to
go further; with the exception, I think, of
Thomas, he is probably the only man of the
primitive band who was originally attracted
to Jesus by the beauty of His moral nature
alone. Neither Peter nor James nor the
other John nor Andrew nor Philip nor
Nathanael seems to have been at first
so attracted; they embraced the hope of a

physical Messiah. But this man cried, 'Behold the Lamb of God!' It was indeed a voice crying in the wilderness. There were very few in the age of Jesus who could appreciate the miracle of a sinless life. Show them a wonderful boy in the home of Nazareth—a boy who can tell thoughts before they are spoken, calculate figures as soon as they are stated, get answers to prayers the instant they are offered—the home of Nazareth will be thronged to suffocation. But tell them that within that house there lives a thoroughly good child, a child of unique goodness—tell them that through all the years of his consciousness he has never been known to depart from a lamblike gentleness, never been seen to deviate from a pure affection, never been observed to waver in an unselfish spirit—you will attract no crowd around the cottage door. The traveller will pause not to wonder, the spectator will wait not to verify; it will seem to the world an ordinary, a commonplace thing.

It is the glory of John the Baptist that he *perceived* the miracle of Nazareth. This man saw the wonder precisely in the one spot where his contemporaries could see nothing. Alone of all the men in the New Gallery this man is first attracted and dominated by that life of Christ which *preceded* outward wonders—His life in the home. He had seen no outpouring of the wine at Cana. He had beheld no cleansing of the temple at Jerusalem. He had witnessed no healing at the pool of Bethesda. He had experienced no glimmer of glory on the Mount of Transfiguration. He had not even listened to the words of wisdom which have immortalised the Hill of Hermon. His vision was only of the child.[1] The spirit of Jesus had to him taken the form of a dove. The kingdom of Christ which *he* had seen was the kingdom over Himself in the nursery. He had marked Him out as the future Messiah on altogether unique grounds. He had demanded a test that could be fulfilled in Nazareth. He had asked no prodigies. He had exacted no feats of prowess.

---

[1] He seems, on account of his desert life, to have lost sight of Him in His manhood; see John i. 33.

He had required no evidence of supernatural knowledge. He had asked sinlessness—a blameless record in the cottage home. By His sustaining of that test, by His ability to pass through that ordeal, the Christ of the Baptist should stand or fall.

I have laid great stress on this point because, if I am not mistaken, we are often prone to take an erroneous view of John the Baptist. We figure a wild man of the woods, half savage and wholly physical—a man whose Christ was of the earth earthy, whose hopes were centred on an outward glory, whose cry was for the carnal, whose faith was in the flesh. We think of him with a kindly patronage—as wonderfully good for the *dawn*. We insist on allowance being made for him. It would be too bad, we say, to compare his rise with the rising of such lights as Peter and the sons of Zebedee. These men saw the Christ full-grown; this man had only the tradition of His *Nazareth*; how can we expect the summer from the spring, why look to dawn for the brightness of the day!

Now, on such an opinion the view I have been advocating falls like a clap of thunder. For, according to my reading of John the Baptist, this representative of the earliest Christianity is the least primitive of all the Christians. So far from contrasting unfavourably with the apostles, he actually begins where they end. The latest word of these apostles is not the outward miracle but the blameless life; it may be said of every one of them that to their autumn years 'the Lamb is all the glory.' But that can be said of the Baptist's spring. He antedated their experience. While they were hunting after a sign of the flesh, he was pursuing a sign of the spirit. While they sought an eagle, he followed the track of a dove. While they waited for the strength of a lion, he placed all his hopes in the spotlessness of a lamb.

The truth is, the original defect of John the Baptist was of exactly the opposite nature to that commonly attributed to him. So far from beginning as a wild man of the woods, the thing he lacked was just the forest freedom. In his morning he was no son of liberty. He had the most exalted view of what it is to be a Christian—a more exalted view than any of his contemporaries; but for that very reason he would make no allowances. He was a red-hot revivalist, and his revivalism admitted no compromise. What he required was not enlightenment; it was expansion. Strange as it may seem, I hold that what all religious youth requires is not enlightenment but expansion. We think of youth as the bird of the wilderness flying reckless from bough to bough and destined to get its wings clipped in the zenith of the day. That is a very good picture of *physical* youth, but it is not religious youth. Religious youth has exactly the opposite development. It is no bird of the wilderness; it is afraid to fly. It is too intense to be broad; it settles on a branch and dwells there. It sees the fire burning in a single bush; it hears the voice calling from only one tree. Its wings may be expected to-morrow, but its weights are for to-day. Its path is a narrow path, its view is a limited view; it sees through a glass darkly and it thinks it sees in full.

There are, in my opinion, two characteristics of the narrowness of religious youth, and they are both found in this figure of the Baptist. The first I would describe as the inability to wait, in other words, a tendency to see the future without intermediate view. This man points to his Christ and cries, 'His fan is in His hand!'—ready to be used. Youth habit-ually scorns the intermediate. It is commonly reckoned a proof of its expansiveness. In truth it is the reverse; it is its inability to fix the eye on any point but one. When a child cries, 'Not to-morrow, nor to-morrow, nor to-morrow, but the next day!' what does it mean? It is really making an attempt to annihilate from its thought the intermediate days as if they were so much useless lumber. That little word 'not' is equivalent to a sup-pression. It declares that the days between Monday and Friday are to be discounted, ignored, put on one side, and that the string of hope should draw the ends so close together as to prevent the impression of anything intermediate at all.

And this is the initial position of John the Baptist. He has a child's inability to wait. His conception of the Messiah is beautiful beyond his time; but his conception of the Messiah's fan is premature. When the hills look too near, there will be rain. I am afraid this great revival preacher is preparing for himself a harvest of tears. It is grandly exciting, no doubt, to see the masses vibrating to the message that the fan is already in the hand. But the fan is in reality not yet within the grasp of the Christ. To the eye of the Baptist the hills look wonderfully near, but the deception will ere long reveal itself. When he stands in the midst of the crowd and cries, 'Behold the Lamb of God!' he is on strong and trenchant ground; but when he predicts the immediate diffusion of the Lamb's purity, he is skating on thin ice. His hearers may be enraptured to-day, but they will be anxious to-morrow and downcast the day after. The Baptist has promised too much. He has held

up the Messiah's winnowing fan in the light
of the coming Sabbath—has held it so as
to exclude the light of all intermediate days.
He has excluded that light from himself as
much as from his hearers. He has taken the
child's leap, that leap which indicates not
breadth but narrowness—the exclusive concentration of the eye upon the lamp farthest
away.

But there is a second characteristic of religious youth, and it also is exemplified in this
great revival preacher. Religious youth is
distinctly uncompromising. It never admits
the possibility of any shades of opinion. A
thing is either white or black, good or bad,
lovely or deformed. This is a tendency, indeed, pertaining more or less to childhood in
general. The average child has no degrees in
his love. His heart is a clock where only two
hours are indicated—twelve noon and twelve
midnight. Ask if he likes any one; you will
get an unqualified yes or no. We are in the
habit of adducing this as evidence of the child's
outspokenness. But in truth the problem lies,

not in speaking out, nor, for that matter, in speaking at all. It lies in the fact that the incipient mind is the imperative mind. I do not think it is a mark of strength, but the reverse; it indicates, not breadth, but narrowness. It implies a limit in judgment, as the previous tendency implied a limit in imagination. It is a mark of crudeness and non-development; yet it is capable of existing side by side with the most exalted idea of purity.

Now, the preacher on the banks of Jordan revealed in pronounced colours this uncompromising spirit of youth. He denied the intermediate shades between night and day. Not only was the Messiah's fan already in the hand; it was to be used drastically. 'He will thoroughly purge His floor, and gather His wheat into the garner; but He will burn up the chaff with unquenchable fire.' The Baptist is in the same position as the servants of Christ's parable. They wanted to consume the tares immediately, 'Wilt Thou that we go and gather them up?' You will remember the answer was, No; and you will remember

why—'Lest while ye gather up the tares ye
root up also the wheat with them.' In nothing
does the wisdom of Christ shine so resplendent
over the wisdom of John. John thought there
were two sets of men—one good and the other
bad; to Christ the good and the bad nestled
in one soul. John thought a fire would do all
that was wanted; Christ feared it might do
more than was wanted. John said, 'If a man
show stubbornness of will, beat it out of him';
Christ cried, 'Not so; you will beat out not
only the stubbornness but the will itself—will
reduce the man to a state of passive imbecility
where decision is hopeless and choice is impossible.' John proposed to kill evil passion
by putting an axe at the root of the tree;
Christ said, 'The root of the tree is not evil
passion but good passion; would you make it
impossible to sin by making it impossible to
feel! would you debar from scenes of badness
by debarring from the sense of sight! would
you cure the temptation of the heart by
making the heart a stone!'

This, then, is the earliest aspect of John

the Baptist—the fiery preacher of a very high Christianity — incapable of compromise, intolerant of middle courses, eager to reduce the outside universe into two hemispheres—heaven and hell! Take a parting look at the man! You will never see him again in this attitude. Something is going to happen, the curtain is about to fall. With all its intolerance, with all its uncompromisingness, with all its repelling severity, there is something in this figure transcendently grand. As it sways to and fro on the banks of Jordan, shaken with the pulsations of its own eloquence—as it breaks forth, now in passionate invective, now in earnest pleading, now in prophetic fervour—I wonder not that the crowds listen and tremble. It is a soul walking on a narrow plank; but on that plank he walks with dauntless foot. The man speaks with conviction; and his conviction is his power. Alone of all the world he has seen the King in His moral beauty—has recognised that lamblike whiteness is better than imperial purple. Basking in that fair ideal of a spotless Christ, he demands a spotless world—demands it now, here, immediately. If the acceptance of Christ meant a change of outward government, men might be allowed to linger; but the acceptance of Christ meant purity, holiness, goodness—all that lies within a man's own heart, ready for the waking touch of God. *This* was a kingdom that needed no armies nor weapons nor fortresses; why should it not come to-morrow, to-day, this hour!

So thought, so spake, John Baptist in the morning. But now, as I have said, the scene is about to vanish. Even as we gaze, the picture melts like snow. Jordan suddenly disappears; the voice of the preacher fades; the crowd upon the bank evaporates as a stream of limelights, and, where the hum of life resounded, universal silence reigns. We are on the borders of a great tragedy—one of the greatest tragedies in history. But what is that tragedy? Perhaps there are few of us who have realised where consists the dramatic horror of the situation. Ask a

Sunday-school child what was the tragedy
that befell John the Baptist, he will answer
without hesitation, ' In the course of his teaching he denounced an illegal marriage of
Herod, who put him in prison and caused
him to be beheaded.' And yet, that is *not*
the dramatic element in the case of the
Baptist. That was a tragedy to the man,
but not to the preacher, not to the reformer,
not to the Christian forerunner. What was
the tragedy to Sir Walter Scott? The loss
of his money? Assuredly not; that might
happen to the most undistinguished man.
But when Scott faded in mind, when his
powers became paralysed, when his right
hand lost its cunning and his mighty brain
ceased to be a highway for the nations, then
came the real tragedy. It was not genius
parting with money; it was genius parting
with itself.

The Baptist's tragedy was analogous to
this. It was not his prison; it was not
his peril; it was not his martyrdom—it was
the fact that he wavered in his first faith.

From the depths of his dungeon he sends a message to the ideal of his dreams, 'Art Thou He that should come, or do we look for another?' Nothing, to my mind, in the whole history of the Baptist is half so tragical as that. And why? Because it is the man parting from his innermost self. It is as if Shakespeare had lost his passion, as if Tennyson had lost his culture, as if Keats had lost his colouring. If this man had kept his confidence undimmed we should have looked in vain for the element of tragedy; not the dungeon, not the persecution by Herod, not the axe of the headsman, could have made the final scene other than glorious. But when a cloud fell over his innermost self, when in the flood he lost sight of the bow, when his *faith* wavered, when his one strong and seemingly invincible possession received damage on a rock of earth—this is the crisis of the drama, this is the tragedy of the scene!

Has the Gallery, then, here committed a breach of art? *Ought* the hero to lose his particular point of heroism? We can understand misfortune, struggle, death; these may only brighten the man's special beauty. But that the special beauty itself should be falsified, that the hero should be untrue to his own soul, that the curtain should fall precisely where his lofty ideal falls—is that a stroke worthy of artistic enthusiasm! Is it not specially *un*worthy of that great Christian art whose aim is not to destroy but to fulfil, and which finds its highest glory when it gathers up the fragments that remain!

In this instance I do not hesitate to answer, No. I say that nowhere has Christianity been more optimistic than in allowing the Baptist's faith to fail. No other stroke would have imparted full glory to the picture. What is it that the Baptist lacks throughout? It is expansion. His taint is narrowness. His ideal of Christ was magnificent, unique among his contemporaries. But he insisted that this ideal should become the immediate possession of the world. He had no place for the wavering, no provision for the stunted, no tenderness for the specially tempted. What this man needed was charity—a deeper sympathy with the infirmities of man. And how was he to get it? How is any man to get it? I know of only one way—he must be depressed in his strong point. Touch him in any other point, and you will fail. But touch him where he is strong, shake him where he has been immovable, and you open the first inlet for the entrance of human charity. The shaking of John's faith was a process preparatory to his spiritual expansion. It prepared him for the answer he was about to receive. He had sent a message to Jesus, 'Art Thou He that should come?' The reply was on the way, and it was virtually an exhortation to remember human frailty. Let me try to paraphrase this reply of Jesus.

'John, it is just because I do not follow your method that I *am* He that should come. Your method is a drastic one. You want to begin by clearing out the chaff. You want me, when I enter the threshing-floor, to look round and be impressed with the absolute purity of all things. You want me to be able to say, " I see no blind here, no lame, no leper, no deaf, no dead in trespasses and sin, no poor and ignorant requiring to be preached to; it is all radiant as a summer day." But, my friend, when I come into the threshing-floor, that is not what I want to see. I wish to see the contrary. I wish to look round and see in the foreground the very men you have put out —the blind, the lame, the leper, the deaf, the spiritually dead, the poor and ignorant. I would have all these cleansed, but I would have them cleansed from the inside. I demand not that the blind should see before they climb the mountain; I ask not that the lame should leap ere they enter by the Beautiful Gate. Let there be no separation between the wheat and the chaff; gather them both into my garner and let me meet them there! Bring in Bartimeus; bring in the man of Bethesda; bring in the typical Magdalene; bring in the leper from the tombs! I shall meet the crowd as they are—unwashed, uncleansed, unbeautified; in their rags and ruin will I give them my hand.'

That is a real paraphrase of the message from Jesus to John. And remember, when it came to John it came to a broken-down man —a man who had been shaken in the sphere of his proudest confidence. What a magnificent preparation for so grand a message! There was a time when John would have scorned to let Bartimeus in; but now his own eye had become dim. There was a time when he would have resented the admission of the man of Bethesda; but now his own feet had become weary. For the first moment in his life he felt himself part of that chaff which he had consigned to everlasting fire. There sprang up in his soul a fellow-feeling with infirmity. The ingathering of the wheat ceased to be the mark of Messianic greatness. To take up tenderly the withered flower, to plant again the fallen tree, to bind the heart that had been wounded, to raise the soul that had been bruised, to give a chance to the reprobate, to find a fresh start for the children of a corrupt heredity, to proclaim a new year in which the darkest life might begin once more—such was that unique ideal of heroism which gave to the dungeon of John's closing days a light of glory which his brightest morning had never known!

I think, then, that the grandest period of the Baptist's life was not the days of his wilderness freedom, but that lonely prison-house from which he only came forth to die. The hour of his physical chain was the hour of his mental enfranchisement. His morning was cribbed, cabined and confined. He was like a man that never had an illness. He had no sympathy with bad health. His besetting weakness was his robust constitution. He could not make allowance for aches and pains, for reaction and weariness. He needed a special gift from God, and that special gift was a privation. Nothing but a privation could set the captive free—could unbar those gates of sympathy whose closure made life to him a desert. But at his evening-time there came that light. It was not the dungeon brought it; it was the shaking of his faith in his own robustness. That shaking was like the cloud on the Mount of Transfiguration. It removed Moses and Elias and revealed Jesus only. The man of law and the man of fire both faded from his horizon, and by his side there stood in undisputed presence the Man of Mercy. Sinai vanished like smoke; Carmel melted like a mimic scene; and, in all the vast expanse, the eye of the great preacher rested on one solitary hill—the love-lit brow of Calvary. With such a vision in his soul the Baptist could afford to die.

L ORD, mine too has been this expansion of the inward life. It is the greatest boon a human heart can know. And yet, my Father, to me, as to the Baptist, it has come through pain. He thought his was an hour of mutilation, of infirmity, of bondage; he bewailed the cloud that had fallen over his faith. But the cloud was sent by *Thee*. Sometimes my faith needs a cloud. I may find it so dazzling that I may be blind to hope and charity. I may cry, 'Destroy the unbelievers, O God; root them out, consume them, annihilate them!' When I say that, Thou sendest my faith a cloud. Thou veilest the heavens over Jordan; Thou hidest the dove descending; Thou utterest no more the voice of the morning. Thou makest me say, 'I see it is a harder thing than I thought to be a believer; I have been too severe upon my brother-man.' I bless Thee for these eclipsing moments, O my God. I bless Thee that I have been touched with the feeling of man's infirmities. I bless Thee that Thou hast put a temporary veil over the face of faith; it has *un*veiled her two sisters—hope and charity. When my sky was cloudless I despaired of those who could not see; when my faith was fearless I was wroth with those who could not believe. But my tremor has made me tender, my mist has made me merciful, my haze has made me human. I have gained more in my night than in my day. In my day I soared beyond sympathy; in my night I caught my brother's hand.   In my day I was solitary on the wing; in my night I had companionship through weakness.   In my day I believed only in the wheat; in my night I had a kindness for the chaff.   In my day I had the feeling of a lonely majesty; in my night I had the fellowship of a common mystery.   It was worth while, O Lord, to wear a chain so golden!

3

John the Self-surrendered

As I pass from the figure of the Baptist I am arrested by two other portraits hanging side by side. The bystanders tell me that they are intended to represent one and the same character—John, Son of Zebedee. One of the portraits, indeed, admits of no doubt on this point; it has the name 'John, Son of Zebedee' appended to it. The other has no title, no inscription; but all the spectators say with one breath, 'That is another likeness of John.' As I look into the faces of these two portraits I am by and by startled—not by their likeness but by their disproportion. They are altogether dissimilar. It is not a question of light hair or dark, pale cheeks or rosy. It is a difference more vital than that—a difference of expression. The professed Son of Zebedee

has an air of self-consciousness about him.
I do not say he is selfish; but he is self-conscious. He is playing a noble part; but he
is aware that he plays it. In a more pronounced sense than Peter he has a tendency
to take the lead. He makes a bid for one of
the two uppermost seats in the Messianic
Kingdom. He takes a portion of Christ's
government into his own hands in the meantime—he interrupts on his own account the
charities of a man who refused to take the
name of Christian. He comes forward as
spokesman when a Samaritan village shuts
its gates—he counsels a return to the old
policy of fire and sword. There are circumstances in his life which are *favourable* to
self-consciousness. He is not so poor as
the other disciples. He has more outlets to
worldly influence than his Galilean brethren—
even the High Priest Caiaphas has a knowledge of him. Above all, he is a mother's
darling—the child of one who rates him far
beyond his present merits, who thinks him
good enough for anything, and who is eagerly

ambitious to advance his interests.[1] There is no mirror which a young man should subject to such close criticism as that which reflects a mother's heart. On the whole, the impression conveyed to my mind by this portrait of the professed Son of Zebedee is that of a misguided and spoiled boy.

But turn now to the other, the nameless picture. It is a complete contrast. If the former was self-conscious, this is self-forgetting. We look into a face whose own look is far away. We feel that we are in the presence of a personality which is almost oblivious of its outward surroundings, altogether oblivious of itself. There is no phrase which to my mind would describe him so well as 'the anonymous man.' It is not only that he never gives his name; he never thinks of his name. In all that he does, in all that he meditates, he keeps hid from himself. The typical attitude in which he is painted is that of a man lying on Christ's bosom. And it truly describes

---

[1] Her ambition, however, was only maternal; her personal attitude to Christ was most unworldly (Matt. xxvii. 56; Mark xv. 40, and xvi. 1).

him. This later portrait is that of one who
rests upon the bosom of humanity. There is
one word which has become his keynote—
brotherhood. The man who in the former
painting asked a private seat above the reach
of the common crowd is found in this later
delineation elbowing his way into the heart
of that crowd and seeking to bury the very
memory of his name in the sense of a life
which made him one with the multitude.

These are the two portraits. What is their
relation to one another ? The bystanders who
first occupied the Gallery were convinced
that they represented one and the same man.
But the modern bystanders have been divided
in opinion. Some have held by the original
spectators—recognising that there may be
two sides to the same character. Others have
been unable thus to bridge the chasm. They
have felt that these two portraits are separated
by the gulf of Dives, that they cannot be
thought of as two sides of a life or two phases
of a character, that they belong to different
atmospheres—one to earth and the other to
heaven—one to the mist over the river, and

the other to the mountain peak lit by the morning sun.

Now, I want to put a question. In point of fact, there is in the New Testament Gallery an instance in which two portraits of the same man are even more pronouncedly different than those attributed to the Son of Zebedee. I allude to the picture of Saul of Tarsus and the subsequent picture of Paul the Apostle. The question I put is this, Why does no one say that *these* cannot represent the same man? Of course the answer will be immediate. You will say, This man, Saul of Tarsus, admittedly turned a somersault; his was a conversion, a transformation, an emergence from darkness into light. And it is quite true that Saul of Tarsus turned a somersault. It is quite true that, as he says himself, he passed through a change equal to that of creation in its emergence from chaos. What is *not* true is the notion that in this transformation of Saul there is anything exceptional. If we exclude John the Baptist, who was in the deepest sense a forerunner, I do not know a man of the Gallery who had not as much need of

transformation as Saul of Tarsus. It is true
he was a persecutor; but negative indifference
is often a bigger gulf than positive opposition.
What separated the Christian and the Jew
was not their hostility; it was their ideas.
The chasm between them was as great ere
ever one opposing voice had been raised on
either side. I must repeat what I have already
said—the New Gallery is not a painting of
qualities but a painting of transformations.
Each is a different transformation; Paul
exhibits one, John exhibits another. If we
allow the double, nay, the contradictory delineation for Paul, why should we not make
the same allowance for John! What we see
in his case is what we see in the case of the
man of Tarsus — transformation. It is the
change from egotism into impersonality, from
consciousness into forgetfulness, from self
into self-surrender. What happened to John
was the breaking of his mirror—the smashing
into fragments of that glass by which he
had shone reflected in his own sight and
had appeared the prime actor in the great
drama.

When did this destruction of the mirror take place? Why should we speak of it as a 'smashing'? Would it not be the result of development? Undoubtedly. But in all development there is one crucial moment— a moment which marks the boundary-line. The building up of individual life is a development—a progress from stage to stage. But there is a special instant in which what we call deadness passes into life. It matters not what theory of life you hold. You may say, if you like, with Herbert Spencer, that it is simply the adjustment of the organism to its environment. Very well. But there is a moment, a crisis moment, in which that adjustment is complete, and in that moment we pass from death unto life. Death in its natural course is also a development—a gradual process of exhaustion. But there is a point in which the process becomes an act, a moment of immediate transformation in which there is no longer any room for development, and in which the change is abrupt, ungraduated, instantaneous—we say, ' The man is dead.'

And John had a crisis moment. It came,
I believe, in that hour when his egotism seemed
to have soared into its climax—when, swayed
by a mother's ambition, he asked the front
seat in the Kingdom.[1] And it was with him
as with Paul—the hour of his deepest moral
need was the hour of his revelation. For a
moment the man of Galilee, like the man
of Tarsus, saw heaven open. And what a
heaven it was! It was a reversal of all his
dreams. In answer to his ignorant and pre-
sumptuous prayer Christ simply raised the
curtain and let the man see in. The sight
which met his gaze paralysed his earthly
wings for evermore; the soaring ceased, the
bird fell. For, what was it he saw—what was
it we all saw? It was a new ideal of greatness. It was not only John the fisherman
who was transformed by that hour. We were
all transformed—kings and senators, empires
and civilisations. The world never got back
to its old régime. What was that old régime?

---

[1] On mature reflection, I would place this incident much
earlier than I did in my *Studies of the Portrait of Christ*.

It was the idea that the greatest man is he who has the million for his servants. But when Jesus said to John, 'Whosoever will be great among you, let him be your minister,' He founded a new régime; He declared that the greatest man is he who is the servant of the million. That the Son of Man—the ideal of all royalty, the synonym for all heroism, should be linked not with mastery but with subordination, that the name to a child of Israel most suggestive of power should be associated with subservience to classes and masses alike, that the life of the potentate should be identified in its deepest essence with a voluntary adoption of the life of the slave—this was not only an epoch-making thought but a thought which has re-moulded all the epochs. We need not wonder that it re-moulded John.

I should say, then, that this was to John the smashing of the mirror. It was his crisis moment. In one of his letters which has always seemed to me to have a ring of autobiography he speaks of having 'passed from death unto life.' Those are the words

of a man who has been *conscious* of a crisis.
They express the sense, not of a process, but
of an act. Doubtless there had been a process too—subtle, hidden, underground; the
greater part of our preparation for the Kingdom is an unconscious preparation. But, as
I have said, to John as to every developing
man there comes a boundary moment, a point
at which the soul must pass over. We may
have a very long walk to the river; but, when
we have reached the river, walking is at an
end—the remainder of the journey is to be
completed by a plunge. John is conscious
of a plunge—of having 'passed over.' He
is conscious of having been on two banks
of the river—of having made the transition
from the bosom of his mother Salome to
the bosom of the Son of Man. He has ex-
changed the love of self for the love of
humanity, ambition for ardour, egotism for
enthusiasm. He feels that the former man
is dead—that death itself could not produce
a greater change. He forgets all the rest
of the process in the transition of a single

moment; and no moment is to my mind so likely as that in which on the plains of earth the Son of Man revealed to him the ideal of heavenly greatness.

But there is one point on which I think many of us have been under a great misapprehension. The popular notion seems to be that John made a transition from a very masculine to a very effeminate nature. I believe it to have been exactly the reverse. I have already expressed the opinion that the influence of John's mother was in the first instance unfavourable to him. He was too much under her tuition and imbibed too much of her spirit. It is a great mistake to imagine that the early petulance and vehemence of John are the mark of a nature not effeminate. They come direct from effeminacy. If the original picture is less gentle than the later picture, it is precisely because it is more effeminate. Those sudden gusts of temper, those sweeping breezes of passion, those eruptions of the lava stream that destroy Samaria and wither even a good man if he refuse to join the Church—whence come they? Just from that which is the root of effeminacy—the absence of self-restraint, the inability to pause and deliberate, the inefficiency of that protective wall which prevents the impulses of the heart from running over.

What John received from his transformation was a virile soul; and it was his virile soul that made his gentleness. I have said that his outburst over Samaria came from the unrestraint of a nature too soft to bind its wrath. But we shall commit a great error if we imagine that the calmness of his after-life came from a suppression of his power to feel. I have no hesitation in saying that there is more evidence of intense and burning feeling in the second picture than in the first. You look at a windless, waveless sea whose surface is unruffled and whose bosom is unclouded. But you do not look long before you find that the stress has been only transferred into the interior. You see heavings below; you hear repressed mutterings underneath; you detect the shadow of a submarine hand holding back the depths with iron grasp and creating the surface calm by the very force of its inward struggle. Listen to the cry that breaks out in one of John's letters!— 'If a man say, I love God, and hateth his brother, he is a liar.' Is that the language of a weakling, of a man emasculated, enervated, emptied of his spirit of fire! Is it not clear that it is the fire which is trying John's work— subjecting him to the crucial test of whether his gentleness has yet made him great, whether he has reached that gift which was absent from his boyhood—the power to be scorched without scorching, to be smitten and not smite!

Do you know what I think the strongest evidence of that self-restraint which became the flower of the Son of Zebedee? It lies, I believe, in something not on the surface, something for which you must read between the lines. There are many moments of love which are not self-restraint, but, in the most sublime sense, self-indulgence. I would not say, for example, that the lying on the Master's bosom was a mark of restraint; I can imagine no greater luxury. I would not say that the standing at the foot of the cross was a mark of restraint; we wonder that the others could restrain themselves from being there. But the fact which I think reveals the transformed John in his summer bloom is his attitude to Judas Iscariot. In nothing does he come so near his Lord. I believe that the only two of the primitive band who detected Judas before the time were John and his Master; upon the rest the betrayal fell like a clap of thunder. John and his Master alone saw the blemish *in the bud.* We know that the Son of Zebedee shared in the perception which had broken upon his Master, because he tells us so. Nobody can read the Fourth Gospel without being impressed with the bitter and implacable loathing which this man by nature entertained for Judas—a loathing more strong, more deep, and more outspoken than is displayed by any of his comrades. This is the fact as it appears on the face of the narrative. The beloved disciple has come

into the dark secret of his Master. He has
detected the blackness in a human soul.
How does he act in these circumstances?
Does he repeat the vituperation that he
launched at the Samaritan village? Does
he call upon the fire to come down and
consume the miscreant? Does he denounce
this man as he denounced the other man for
working in a Name he did not worship? No;
he has learned self-restraint now. He con-
ceals his revelation. He meets Judas as he
meets Peter. He meets him at the council,
he meets him at the feast, he meets him in
that solemn hour sacred to the coming bereave-
ment—the hour of all others when we sigh for
kindred souls. He meets him, he greets him,
as a brother; he represses the pent-up fury
of his heart.

The question is, Why? I have said it was
self-restraint; but the question still remains
—Why? There is no such thing in Christianity as self-restraint for its own sake. It is
not a Christian virtue; it is a Stoic virtue.
There are hundreds who have passed through

the fiery furnace and never revealed that they got any hurt; the mind can be taught to suppress its cries. But Christian self-restraint is not suppression; it is surrender. I may keep back my cry from pride, or I may keep back my cry because I have seen a possibility of succour. John's attitude to Judas is the latter of these. Why does he treat him as a brother? Because in the companionship of the Master he had awakened to the sense of brotherhood, As long as the shell had not burst, John and his Master had a ray of hope for Judas. Did you ever ask yourself the reason of Christ's open proclamation of the prophecy, 'One of you shall betray me.' 'To show His miraculous power,' you say. What I regard as an unhappy gloss has put that reason into Christ's mouth; but He Himself would have repudiated it. It required no miraculous power to see through Judas, nor was there any miracle in the vision. I ask again, therefore, Why does Christ in the presence of Judas himself keep ringing the changes of the prophecy, 'One of you shall betray me'? And I answer,

' It is in the hope that the prophecy will not come true.' He wants the man to take fright at the mirror of himself—as David did when he was painted by Nathan, as Nineveh did when it was pictured by Jonah. If by any chance he could *see* himself—if for him, bad as he was, lurid as he was, repulsive as he was, there could lurk in some corner, however small, the tiniest patch of green—if any stray word could waken him, any chance light scorch him, any sudden snapshot reveal him to himself—the Master would be proud that His prophecy should fail.

Now, I believe Christ's first work for the transformed John was the bearing with Judas. When he had reached the spiritual shore— that state which, though on earth, he called the world beyond death—the first work that awaited him was a reversal of his past. As an arrogant youth, he had called upon the flames to wrap round and round the walls of a Samaritan village that had closed its gates on Jesus. But here was a spectacle compared to which the guilt of Samaria's village grew

pale! Here was a *life* closing its gates—body
and soul, nerve and sinew, heart and brain;
here was a mind so dark, so irresponsive, so
unsympathetic that John himself in a moment
of self-communion calls him the 'son of perdition'![1] But a voice says: 'Do not accelerate
the perdition; do not anticipate the perdition;
give the man a chance—a chance in your own
heart! Do not let the fire come down upon
Samaria even in imagination! Keep it away
from your fancy; hope against it; pray against
it; love against it! I do not say, "Restrain
yourself, curb yourself, control yourself!"—I
would rather prescribe the wing than the
chain. Bathe yourself in brotherhood, lave
yourself in love, hide yourself in humanity,
sun yourself in the service of man; and you
will no more need to pray, "Keep back my
angry soul!"'

Here is a fitting place to bid John farewell
—in that haven of love which was to him the

[1] I believe the words, 'None of them is lost, but the son
of perdition' to be John's passing comment on the statement
of Christ's prayer, 'Those that Thou gavest me I have kept'
(John xvii. 12).

other side of death. Three times, in the testimony of after-days, the curtain rises on the man. Very surprising to me are these successive risings. Viewed as historical or viewed as traditional, they mark the true sequence of the spiritual life. Life has ever three typical periods; I would call them the age of imagination, the age of reason, and the age of simplicity. We all begin with our Apocalypse—our sight of a city of gold with pearly gates and crystal fountains and nightless skies. We do not move *forward* through life; we move backward. The first thing we see is the drama completed. The dawn that greets the eye of youth is not the dawn of its own morning but the dawn of futurity. Yesterday has no power, to-day has no power; we light our torch at the sun of to-morrow. Then comes the second step, and it is a step backward. We fall into the *present* world. Reason takes the place of imagination. To-morrow fades in to-day. Instead of looking forward we look round. We begin to ask, Who are we?—Where are we?—What is the cause of our

being?—Why are there so many streets that
are *not* golden, so many gates that are *not*
of pearl, so many skies that are *all* night?
By and by there comes a third and final stage.
It is what we should have expected to come
first—the *past* of the man. He ends where
we should have looked for him to begin—in
the simplicity of a child. Arguments lose
their interest; theories cease to trouble; ques-
tionings are not long harboured in the mind
—after the days of tracing come the days of
trusting.

And these are the curtains that rise over
the subsequent life of John. We see the
heart of youth swelling with the anticipation
of future glories—the man of the Apocalypse,
the man of Patmos. Then we see the heart
of maturity—the sober, grave, and reverent
senior, living entirely in the problems of his
age, and striving to mould philosophy into
the image of his Christ; it is the man of re-
search, the man of the Fourth Gospel. At last
there comes the final raising of the curtain;
and we see a little child. He has gone back

to the past. We have a series of charmingly simple letters which make the close of his life a tribute to the instincts of childhood. The harp of youth may have lost most of its strings, the accents of philosophy may have ceased to charm ; but there is one primitive word that dominates, rules, over-rules—it is 'love.' That word—the child's first medium of revelation—becomes to this old man the one test of all spiritual beauty, the one proof that God is true, the one unassailable evidence of the destiny and the mission of man.

MY Father, when I look at Thy Great Gallery of Christian souls, it brings a deep comfort to my heart to know that they were not *always* beautiful. If theirs had been a native splendour, I should have sunk beneath the glow. But I bless Thee that these beautiful faces have been gifts from *Thee*. I bless Thee that in the opening of their lives they were so very plain. It is not a prodigy that gives me hope ; it is a dull boy rising to

distinction. Even so, my hope of loveliness
is when I see beauty come from unpromising
soil. I thank Thee that Thou hast let me
see the dust of the earth out of which came
the beloved disciple—the egotism, the vanity,
the worldly ambition, the forgetfulness of
others, the unrestrained passion, the dictatorial
pride, the mirror of self-consciousness filling
all the heart. It is an unholy picture; but
it makes me throb with the promise and
potency of holiness. For, this is the man who
summers in the bowers of eternal beauty—in
the haven of cloudless love! This is the man
that rests on the bosom of Thy fair Christ!
He has climbed from rags into radiance. He
has soared from dust into divinity. He has
mounted from the shadow into the sunshine.
Therefore, my Father, there is hope for me—
not of bare salvation, but of the glory of an
archangel. I too may bask in Thy heights;
I too may dwell in Thy nightless skies. Only
let Thy Christ stand over my dust, and it
will bloom. One sight of Him will break the
mirror of my vanity. One touch of Him will

still the beatings of my ambition. One tone of Him will give my passions calm. One sigh of Him will shatter all my pride. One memory of Him will make me remember myself no more. Transform me by Thy Christ, O my God!

4

Nathanael the Invigorated

As we advance through the Great Gallery
we are confronted by a face which has left
its impress on the canvas of all time; it is
that of Nathanael. There are three voices
in the verb 'to live'—being, doing, suffering.
There are some who come into this world to
'do'; they are sent to work out a mission.
There are some who come into this world
to 'bear'; their special gift from God has
been a thorn. But there are a few who are
sent neither to do nor to bear, but simply to
'be.' Nathanael belongs to the last class.
If you ask what he did, I cannot tell. I can
tell what Peter did, what John did, what Paul
did—but not what Nathanael did. His mission
was his being, and his being was his beauty.

We feel as if we were watching a child whose years are to be few, and for whom there is no active work designed, yet whose petals we see unfolding and whose buds we behold expanding. The picture of Nathanael is strictly the unfolding of a flower. We are accustomed to say that we are told nothing about him. Nothing of what he did, nothing of what he bore—but of what he was, a whole biography! Come and unfold the flower with me as it grows under the fig-tree! It is the only life in the New Testament Gallery which is revealed emerging from rustic scenes. Peter, Andrew, James, the apostle John, probably Philip, rise from the sea. Matthew issues from the exchange. Mark comes from a secretary's room. Nicodemus seems to have come out of a library. But Nathanael emerges from under a fig-tree.[1] He is the rustic of the primitive band. Rusticity is the first stage of his life-flower. A native of Cana in Galilee, he has never left that village for any contact

---

[1] It is possible, in the light of John xxi. 2 and 3, that at an after-date he joined the fisherman's craft.

with a busy town. He has not rubbed with
the world, and he remains still an artless child
—free from scheming, free from ambition, free
from jealousy, free from the consciousness
of self. He is without vices; but as yet it
is only the faultlessness of rustic simplicity.

I think we are in a great mistake about the
meaning of these words which Jesus spoke
of Nathanael, 'Behold an Israelite indeed, in
whom is no guile.' As popularly understood,
they would be a eulogium fit to emblazon on
the wings of angel or archangel, cherub or
seraph. If Nathanael has reached this altitude,
why call him to Jesus at all! Could Christ
do more for any man than make him free
from guile! If this man has reached the
climax, he has no need of the climbing; the
ladder from earth to heaven is in his case
quite superfluous! Let him remain under the
fig-tree and meditate on his own skies; he
can see no greater things than these!

But my reading of this passage is very
different. I would paraphrase it thus: 'It is
not opposition I am afraid of; it is dishonest

opposition. I see a man resting under a tree. He is a thorough Israelite—earnestly devoted to the Rabbinical traditions of his country, and therefore naturally not in sympathy with me. Yet in his opposition there is no guile. There is nothing mean about it, nothing personal, nothing paltry. He is genuinely afraid of the new movement—afraid from the highest, purest motives. There *will* be an opposition which will come from guile. Men will refuse to come to me through fear of the cross, through dread of the sacrifice which my religion involves. But here is a man who is afraid he will *lose* the cross, afraid he will be deprived of the *chance* of sacrifice. He says, "Can any good thing come out of Nazareth!" He thinks my religion will be too gay a thing, too sportive, too joyous. He distrusts Nazareth, he distrusts any part of Galilee. Galilee is too near the Gentiles for him—too near the confluence of the sinful nations who spend their life in eating and drinking, marrying and giving in marriage. He fears it will be a worldly religion, withdrawing the mind from what is serious and making the faith of Israel an imitation of the games of Greece.'

Consider, for a rustic like Nathanael and one with the weakness of a rustic, there was nothing strange in his entertaining such a presentiment. For let us remember that Christianity is the only religious revival in the world which has come in gay attire. Everywhere else the revival of religion has appeared in dust and ashes; men have beat upon their breasts and cried, 'Unclean!' Christ Himself was at first disposed to fast; but He had changed His thought—changed it for the ringing of bells and the playing of dance-music. And the sequel was to emphasise the change. Any man of the Baptist's school would be startled out of his senses by what he was to see. He would see Jesus Himself immediately after His opening ministry[1] providing for the supply of wine at a marriage feast! He would see this same Jesus turning a religious meeting into a social picnic because He saw that the people were faint and weary! He would see Matthew

---

[1] John's first chapters presuppose that Christ was in the air *previous* to the feast of Cana.

signalising his conversion by a sumptuous dinner to his friends! He would see young ministers after the Sunday-morning service walking in the fields and plucking the ears of corn! He would see Martha—not in spite of, but by reason of, Christ's presence—spreading the richest repast that ever graced a table in Bethany! All this he would be compelled to view.

And what would he feel? Very much, I think, what a former generation of simple country-people felt when the innovations of modern science first broke upon the scene. When the white sail was supplanted by the black wreaths of the steamer; when the shrill railway-whistle woke the silent air; when a message was sent to India and an answer came back within an hour; when a man was told that he could speak to his brother through a distance of sixteen hundred miles; when, later still, the voices of men were bottled up in jars, carried across the Atlantic, and made to deliver speeches or sing songs after perhaps their original owners had passed away from earth—I say, such revelations as these must have shaken all the lives reposing under the fig-tree. They must have felt as if private communion were abolished, as if the life of public day had extinguished for ever the possibilities of the quiet hour, as if there were no longer a meeting-place between the soul and God.

I have attributed to Nathanael the weakness of the rustic. Some may be shocked by the ascription. But to me it is an impossible supposition that Jesus had any need to convert a man who was already in the literal sense holy, harmless, undefiled. Christ came to transform ; if Nathanael was perfect, there was nothing to change in him. I think there *was* something to change. I believe that originally his understanding was narrow; he wanted mental vigour, and Christ called him to give him that vigour. To me the want of mental vigour appears more in the second stage of the flower than in the first. It is not so much in his *opposition* to Christ as in his acceptance of Christ that the weakness is seen. If he was opposed to Christ on inadequate evidence, he accepted Him on evidence more inadequate still. The narrative is given in very direct and simple terms, and may be briefly recapitulated.

Philip runs into Nathanael's retreat and accosts him with the virtual announcement, 'The Messiah is come — the long-expected, the long-desired; He is come in the person of a toiling man, a man of Nazareth!' 'That cannot be,' cries Nathanael; 'we who are of Galilee know too much about its sinfulness to recognise a Christ from Nazareth!' 'Instead of arguing about the matter,' exclaims Philip, 'come and see for yourself; look at the man with your own eyes, and judge him!' Nathanael agrees to the test. He is brought right into the presence of Jesus. Jesus greets him as one with whom He had long been familiar. 'How do you know me?' says Nathanael. Jesus answers, 'I saw you sitting under the fig-tree before any man's attention was directed to you.' Then, with a great rush of enthusiasm, with a gust of conviction that swept all before it, Nathanael breaks forth into the vehement exclamation,

'Rabbi, Thou art the Son of God, Thou art the King of Israel!'

Now, I have no hesitation in saying that the rustic was prominent here. Nathanael had entered upon a great sea in a boat that was not fit to bear a single gale. The conclusion was far too big for the premises. He had rested the Messiahship of Jesus on what would now be called an act of clairvoyance— a power to see things at a distance. That was no mark of Messiahship; I doubt if it was even a necessary mark of goodness. It was a possession of the prophets—and there were bad men with the prophetic faculty. So far as I see, all the wicked people in Nazareth might have had this power without in the slightest degree diminishing their wickedness. Nathanael was here untrue to that fine moral bias which had prompted his original prejudice. The moral bias was the one good thing about the prejudice. He was then in search of *goodness* from his Christ; it was a terrible fall to come down to clairvoyance. Jesus Himself was surprised at the crude conviction. 'Because I said I saw thee under the fig-tree, believest thou!' It is not the glad surprise He expressed later at the faith of the Phœnician woman. He recognises, no doubt, that Nathanael has made an advance—that the flower has actually found its way into the light; but He feels that it has dropped something in the process. Nathanael has lowered his demand. He has abated his claim. He has consented to take less from his Christ than he asked under the fig-tree. There, he had demanded a Christ who should come from a holy soil, whose environment should be solemn, whose tread should be serious. Now, he has for the time forgotten these impressions, and is willing to reverence a King who has the attribute of second sight!

Let us understand this matter. The Christ of the Gospels desires beyond all things to secure proximity to Himself. He will accept that on any terms—even should the coming be for the sake of the loaves; He knows that mere proximity will eventually kindle fire.

But in the case of such inadequate motives there is absent an element of joy. It is not that there is little faith. I believe Nathanael had enormous faith. I believe he would have gone to the stake for his faith. I think his conviction at that moment was deeper than that of any of the previous converts—deeper than Peter's or John's or Philip's or Andrew's. But the conviction itself was based on something which Christ did not hold to be an essential part of His system. Let me try to illustrate the difference between the 'little faith' and the 'inadequate faith.'

Imagine that a popular plebiscite were taken with the view of ascertaining the public's estimate of some great poet—let us say, Robert Browning. Let us suppose that hundreds of sheets were crowded with panegyrics and a few tens with adverse criticisms. But let us conceive the idea that the list was closed by two very unique statements of opinion, neither of which could be described as either eulogy or blame, and which by their very eccentricity excited much attention. Let

us imagine the contents of these two para-
graphs. We begin with the last but one.

It says : 'I believe that Browning has a
power which I have not perceived. His *great*
poems are quite obscure to me. I cannot
understand *Sordello* ; I cannot fathom *Para-
celsus* ; I cannot unravel *The Ring and the
Book*. I must say, with the Psalmist, "Such
knowledge is too great for me ; it is high ; I
cannot attain unto it." Yet I am willing to
believe that the error is in *me*. The reason
is that when I read some of his small pieces,
such as *Evelyn Hope* and *Easter Day*, I feel
charmed both with thought and style. These
fragments enliven me, refresh me, quicken me.
I would come to Browning for these tiny
sparks from the anvil. The great work of
his forge is meaningless to me ; but the
sparks have light and warmth, and they seem
to beckon me on to the hope of higher vision.'

Now, I should say that this man had 'a little
faith' in Browning. He believes in him to the
extent of *Evelyn Hope* and *Easter Day* ; and on
account of that belief he distrusts his adverse

judgment of the rest. These are elements of faith—very few, very fragmentary, very simple, but pointing in the right direction. Let us look now at the other and latest paragraph; it breathes a sentiment wholly different, and must be measured by a standard of its own.

It says: 'I am sure that Browning is a born poet. I have never read him, but I have done better—I have come into contact with his soul. I was privileged once to meet him, to be introduced to him. It was under a tree. I had run beneath its branches for shelter from a passing shower, and there I found a group already gathered, of whom Browning was one. He was made known to me; and it seemed as if he had known me all along. His manner was that of a familiar friend. Nothing could exceed his courtesy, his urbanity, his freedom from self-consciousness, his personal interest in the things of which I spoke. I felt then and I feel now that only the soul of a poet could have enabled any man to throw himself thus into the life of another.'

I ask, What is the position of this man? Is he in want of faith? No; he has boundless faith; he has crowned his ideal with full laurels. But then, it is Nathanael's crown— a crown given for inadequate causes. He has accepted Browning as his laureate, not on account of his poetry, but on account of an interview under a tree. He has reached a royal conclusion by faulty premises. No doubt it is good that in any capacity he should stand near Browning. We will not rob him of his place; hereafter he may bloom by reason of the contact. We only claim the right to say that he has reached this place by a short and easy method, and that he will some day have to fall back to conquer the unappropriated ground.

And now I come to the third and final step in the spiritual history of Nathanael. It is announced by Jesus as something still in the future which is awaiting him and all of them; but it is announced as a positive certainty— with the formula, 'Verily, verily, I say unto you.' Jesus predicts Nathanael's mental in-

vigoration.   He predicts the time when he
will base His claims on something higher than
a case of physical clairvoyance—'You shall
see heaven open, and the angels of God
ascending and descending upon the Son of
Man.'

What does this mean?   Literally it says,
'You Nathanael, and the rest of you, will
yet see the fulfilment of Jacob's vision.'   But
what was Jacob's vision?   It was the vision
of God's charity to man.   The angels are
ascending and descending for purposes of
ministration; they are the ministrant spirits
of the old dispensation.   But there is one
statement of Christ which is an addition to
the picture, and which is to my mind strik-
ingly original.   It is the words, 'upon the
Son of Man.'   I do not think we have grasped
the significance of these words.   Jesus claims
charity as the special evidence of His religion.
He says that He is the basis of all philanthropy, of all benevolence, of all humanitarian
effort.   He refuses the name of charity to
anything which does not move 'on the steps

of the Son of Man.' He tells Nathanael that this, and not clairvoyance, is to be the sign of His Messiahship. He claims to be the founder of active sympathy; on His steps alone could it descend from heaven; other foundation could no man lay.

Consider. In the world before Christ, in the world into which Christ was born, charity had sought to descend by the steps of other ladders. The Stoic had preached forgiveness of injury; but the ladder on which he descended was the sense of contempt for man. Nobody was worth being angry at, nobody was worth quarrelling with. The mass of the human race were poor creatures, too insignificant to stir dissension in the breast of a philosopher or wake revenge in the soul of a thinker. Again. The Roman supported institutions for the healing of wounded soldiers and the cure of sick slaves; but the ladder on which he descended was the spirit of self-interest. He wanted to preserve his property. If the soldier had the prospect of life in him, he might again serve his country; if the slave gave hope of recovery, he might again serve his master. The hospitals of that old world were not homes for the good of the sufferer; they were homes for the good of the healthy. They were intended to recruit the sinews of war for the leaders of armies; they were designed to recoup the resources of wealth for the masters of households. Do I speak this to their blame? Assuredly not. It was an aim legitimate and right. But it was not the vision which Nathanael was to see. It was not a descent on the steps of the Son of Man. In fact, man had nothing to do with it; he was the one factor absent from human calculation. Nobody took into account that he was lying on a bed of pain; nobody asked whether his suffering could be mitigated. The one question was, Could it be cured? — could he be made available for the economy of the state or the economy of the domestic hearth? If he could, the gates of the infirmary were thrown open to him; if he could not, he had the fate of the man at the Pool of Bethesda—he could not get in.

Now, Nathanael's vision was to be very
different from this. The difference lay in the
medium of descent. Rome stooped from her
proud altitude to bind the wounds of the
sufferer; but the ladder on which she came
was not the ladder of Jacob—she descended
on the steps of self-interest. But the steps
of the Son of Man led in the opposite way.
There was no thought of self, no thought of
personal damage, no thought of lost service.
There was only one thought—that a human
form was being mutilated, that a human heart
was feeling sad. Even the possibility of recovery was not the boundary-line of sympathy.
Man's physical care was to go beyond his
physical hope. It was to take up the incur-
ables. It was to provide a home for those who
would serve no more, would fight no more,
would be citizens of their country no more.
It was to prepare for them a new citizenship
—a place where they could abide under the
shadow of the Almighty and render obedience,
not in serving, but in waiting. This was the
spectacle which in the days to come was to

greet the eyes of Nathanael. And the strange thing is that the ground of this compassion for human suffering was not the insignificance but the greatness of man. Not because he was a poor, helpless creature shaken by every wind and at the mercy of every circumstance was man's benevolence to be evoked for man. Rather was charity to be elicited by the fact that above the manger there was a star, that in company with the weary night-vigils there were choirs of celestial song, that, lying beside the impotence of the babe, there were gold and frankincense and myrrh that told of a coming glory.

Before taking leave of Nathanael there is one thing I should like to say. Christian writers, as a rule, have been eager to include his name in the list of the twelve apostles— they have tried to identify him with Bartholomew. It has seemed to them that one so early called *must* have been an apostle. In that view I cannot concur. I do not think Nathanael was an apostle. I believe the Fourth Gospel had for one of its designs just to show that men could get close to Jesus without any official position. Look at its very keynote!—'As many as received Him, to them gave He power to become the sons of God, even to them that believe on His name.' That keynote seeks to show that on the wings of inward faith, whose beating is inaudible even to the bystander, the humblest soul may soar direct into the heart of the Master. Accordingly, this Gospel has a record regarding Christians elsewhere unnamed or undwelt on — Nathanael, Nicodemus, Martha, Mary, Lazarus. Every one of them was brought as near to Jesus as any apostle of the band. Nathanael saw His glory; Nicodemus buried Him; Mary anointed Him; Martha reasoned with Him; Lazarus rose with Him in resurrection life. To be in such a company was worth all the privileges of the twelve.

SON of Man, they tell me that Thy crown has faded. They are wrong; it was never so bright as now. To Thee there was

ever but one crown—Charity; to this end
wert Thou born and for this cause camest
Thou into the world. Men have mistaken the
nature of Thy glory. Like Nathanael, they
have seen Thy lustre in a bauble; and when
the bauble has broken they have said that
Thou hast faded. But in truth Thou hast
had to wait for Thy glory, O Christ; it is only
fully in sight now. Charity is the youngest-
born child of Thy Father. There have been
days of prophecy, days of eloquence, days of
doctrine, days of creed and confession; but
charity was still a child. It is but yesterday
that we have begun to descend on Thy steps;
but at last the dawn is breaking! Above the
creed there has sounded the cry—the cry of
wounded humanity. We used to ask how we
were to ascend with Thee to heaven; we are
now inquiring how we are to descend with
Thee to earth. We cannot get deep enough
down until we get into Thy chariot; our
brother's rags are too loathsome to us till we
have sight of *Thee*. But Thou hast heightened
my helpfulness by heightening my standard of

man. It is not pity that I need; it is praise. It is not tears that I need; it is triumph. It is not heaviness that I need; it is hope. Others can show me the vile raiment of the prodigal; Thou pointest to the robe that is awaiting him. Others can tell me he is despised; Thy look follows him afar off. Others with a passing tear can leave him among the swine; Thou preparest for him the music in the house of the Father. Take us into Thy descending chariot, O Son of Man!

5

Peter the Emboldened

THERE is no figure in the New Testament Gallery which presents to the eye such a mixture of simplicity and enigma as that of Simon Peter. To outward appearance his character may be read on the surface. He is not a theologian like John the Baptist; he is not a mystic like John the Evangelist; he is a plain, blunt man that speaks the language of the common day and breathes the wants of the passing hour. He is more like an open book than is any other figure in the Gallery. We feel that we have met him often, that we shall meet him many times again. He is one of those men who on a superficial view promise to offer a very easy subject of study. And yet the promise is a delusion. Among the spectators of that

Gallery there has been probably more disagreement about the character of Simon Peter than about the character of any other representative of New Testament life. It very often happens that the men and women we meet in this world who seem most open and above-board are precisely those who prove the most difficult to read. Simon Peter is one of these. He not only seems, but he is, above-board. There is nothing sinister, nothing secret, nothing underhand ; his words and deeds convey exactly the meaning he intends them to convey. Yet at the close of our inspection we find ourselves entangled in what appears to be a web of inconsistencies from which there is no hope of extrication. We seem to be confronted by a life of opposing qualities—sometimes touching the heavens, at others coming perilously near the nether world—now in the heights of ecstasy, anon in the depths of despair—to-day winning our admiration, to-morrow exciting a feeling akin to repulsion. The life, in fact, alternates between cowardice and bravery. These are

the poles betwixt which he wavers. Every
great thing he does comes from a moment
of bravery; every mean act to which he
stoops comes from a moment of cowardice.
The most cursory examination will make this
clear.

The symbol of his whole life is the sea-
walking. That is in miniature the picture
of his entire character. We see him for an
instant on the top of the wave, daring a
deed which none of his compeers could have
dared; the next he is shrieking with abject
terror, 'Lord, save me!' And the picture
gives no outward cause for this. We see
no increase of the storm. The wind has not
heightened; the waves have not swollen; the
sea does not look more scowling than when
he planted his foot upon its bosom. It is
a struggle pure and simple between bravery
in his own breast and cowardice in his own
breast. And this picture, as I have said, is
the keynote to every incident of his life.
He makes professions of loyalty to Jesus far
beyond those of his brethren; in an hour of

real danger he shows the courage to maintain them—he draws a sword in the garden against heavy odds. Yet within a few hours this man quails before the question of a servant-girl, and denies the Lord whom he loves! I see again no adequate cause for the change; it must have come from a tremor in his own soul. Once more. He was one of the first to recognise the claims of the Gentiles. Bravely did he stand forth as the champion of Gentile freedom at a time when the thought was exciting deep animosities. For ventilating that thought Stephen had paid the penalty with his life. For ventilating that thought the convert Paul had been forced to retire into temporary exile. It was at such a moment that Peter's voice was raised in courageous vindication of a universal Gospel. Yet, within a few brief years, this same man goes down to Antioch, and in the face of far less danger keeps aloof from the Gentile converts! Again I say I fail to recognise an adequate outward cause for the change. The cause, whatever it is, is *within* the man.

His soul is a battlefield between bravery and cowardice; and here contend for the mastery of his heart the two most opposite things in life—the heroism of the soldier and the abjectness of the poltroon.

Here, then, is a subject for the psychologist. We want to know why it was that within the soul of this man there could dwell such conflicting elements. We can understand a mixture of doubt and faith, we can imagine a union of weakness and strength, we can comprehend the existence of a natural placidness side by side with the possibility of flashing fire; but the co-existence of bravery and cowardice, the union of the hero and the faint-heart — that is something which challenges the philosopher and calls for explanation.

Let me begin by giving the *popular* explanation. It is this: 'Peter is set forth as an example of the principle, "Let him that thinketh he standeth take heed lest he fall." He is a monument of the fact that men are liable to fail in their strongest qualities unless

periodically renewed by Divine Grace. Peter
was by nature a brave man. He possessed
a soul of fire which made him forget his own
limitations, which drove him instantaneously
into work beyond his power. He lived by
confidence in his own strength, and he over-
rated his own strength. He was one of those
men to whom preliminary success is necessary. If his first charge were successful, he
would carry all before him. But if checked
in the assault, he would sink suddenly, utterly,
ignominiously. All his courage would desert
him. A great reaction would come, in which
the once powerful heart would become prostrate, in which the spirit ready to dare all
things would bow itself to the dust—convey-
ing the moral to all self-confident souls that
the highest human gift needs to be supported
from above.'

Now, without for a moment disputing the
truth of the moral, this is not my view of
the character of Simon Peter as delineated
in the Gospel Gallery. I must repeat that
this Gallery is a record of transformations, in

which each man passes from a lower into a higher self. But the view here adduced would make Peter's higher self the original element and his later self the decline. The whole picture, as I take it, is based upon an opposite conception. Instead of being by nature the courageous man we portray, the Peter of the Gallery is introduced to us as a man of extreme timidity—one of those trembling, shrinking souls that suggest rather the girl than the youth. We shall go wrong, in my opinion, if we do not start from this basis. I admit that we are dealing with an inconsistent character ; but let us not mistake the nature of the inconsistency. The inconsistency of Peter lies in his strength and not in his weakness. The inconsistency is the *Divine* thing about him—the thing that brings him nearest to his Master. It lies not in the fact that a brave man periodically becomes a coward, but that a cowardly man periodically becomes brave. It is as if a miser were suddenly to give an enormous subscription to a charitable institution ; the subscription, and not the miserliness, is the thing to be accounted for. Our wonder should begin, not where Peter sinks, but where he stands upon the wave—not where he denies his Lord, but where he vows to die with Him. To take such a view is not only more consonant with the picture, it is really more just to Peter. It places his character on a higher level. To fall from an original eminence implies a moral stain; but to rise to a height which you have not yet acquired the adequate strength to maintain—this is but a sign of weakness, and ought to be a ground of sympathy.

From this point of view I should be disposed to divide the life of Peter into three periods. The first is the time when timidity reigns supreme. The second is the stage in which there begins a struggle between timidity and a new principle—courage. The third is that period in which the new principle vanquishes the old and courage becomes the dominant note of his life.

First, then. Peter originally appears in an

attitude of constitutional timidity. You say, Was he not a fisherman—one who is supposed to buffet the winds and the waves and look with scorn upon the elements of danger! Yes; and has it never struck you with surprise that the earliest instance of timidity we meet in the Gospels is just among Christ's little band of fishermen—of whom Peter was one! I have often marvelled that when that squall burst upon the bark on the Sea of Galilee these men manifested such abject trepidation. Fancy a company of English sailors overtaken by a sudden gale and giving vent to their feelings in a simultaneous shriek of terror—' Save us, we perish!' But it is precisely such a fancy that explains the mystery. For, these men are not English; they are at the opposite remove from the Englishman. The fishermen of England, the mariners of England, the very tourists of England, have become so endeared to the sea that even its storms bring a sense of exhilaration. But to the son of Judah the sea was always a horror. Jonah was no exceptional case when he ran to sea to escape the presence of the Lord God. It was to all his country-men the one region where the presence of the Lord God could not be traced. Although the exigencies of daily life demanded from the men of Galilee the prevalence of the fisher-man's calling, I do not think it was for them a voluntary profession. I think the fishermen were the most timid set of the community— as the shepherds were the bravest. I have no doubt they went out into the deep with fear and trembling, inquired anxiously the signs of the sky, experienced during the voyage all the palpitations of the shrinking heart, and thanked God fervently when they encountered no gale. ' We have left all, and followed Thee,' said Peter to the Lord, speaking for himself and his fellow-fishermen. But in truth neither he nor they had made any sacrifice. They were very glad to get rid of their calling on the chance of something else. That 'some-thing else' was precarious; but the sea was more precarious still. We err if we imagine that these men left a comfortable living. They

left a struggling, and, to their mind, a dangerous, mode of subsistence—a life which heredity
had made full of unpleasant associations, and
which the national instinct shrank from.   It is
written of Christ that He once '*constrained* His
disciples to get into a ship'; that is what life's
struggle always did to the men of Galilee.

Peter carried his lack of courage into the
kingdom. He left his boat behind him, but
he left not behind him his timidity. Christ
took men into His kingdom with their old
garments on; the ring and the robe were
an after-consideration. He let them come
with all the elements of their imperfection
clinging round them — with the hand un-
ringed, with the feet unshod, with the vesture
unadorned. Within His holy temple the
votaries again and again revealed traces of
old culture—the remains of a former day.
There are incidents in Peter's life which are
commonly attributed to bold presumption, but
which, to my mind, suggest only the survival
of this primitive culture—the spirit of extreme
timidity. Take that memorable occasion on

which the Master broke to His disciples the
tidings of His approaching death and when
Peter exclaimed with hot repudiation, 'Be it
far from Thee, Lord; this will not be unto
Thee!' It is commonly set down to his
impertinent forwardness. I think it was the
voice of shrinking fear. No doubt devotion to
Jesus counted for something; but they were
all devoted as well as Peter. We have to find
a reason why Peter was the spokesman. And
I think that reason lay, not in his being the
most impertinent, but in his being the most
timid. He shrank from the thought of danger.
He sought to figure a brighter destiny. With
a sailor's superstition, he cried out against the
omen as if he would avert it, bear it down.
He is an object rather for compassion than for
recrimination. Will it be said that the sternness of Christ's reproof, 'Get thee behind me,
Satan!' is at variance with such a view? But
to whom was that reproof administered? To
Peter? No—to Satan—to the tempter of the
wilderness. We are told that after the temptation Satan left Him 'for a season.' This im-

plies that he was to come back. He had come
back now, and he had come back with the old
temptation—to reject the cross for the crown,
to choose the purple instead of the poverty,
to sway by law in place of stooping by love.
It was not to Peter that Christ administered
the rebuke. It was not Peter that He saw
before Him ; it was the tempter once more—
that tempter whom He had already similarly
and summarily dismissed. The disciple who
had just been commended for having a revelation which flesh and blood had not communi-
cated would never have been addressed by
the name of 'Satan'!

There is another incident commonly attributed to the presumption of Peter which I
think has its source in his timidity. I allude
to that moment on the Mount of Transfiguration when he exclaimed, 'Methinks it is good
to be here ; and let us make three tabernacles
—one for Thee and one for Moses and one for
Elias!' The dictation of a plan to Jesus is
startling enough ; but I think it was really a
cry of fear. The refrain of that death-prophecy

was still ringing in his ears. He attributed to Jesus the dream of a Messianic conquest. He thought, if that dream could be dispelled, the death and danger prefigured would melt away. If, instead of battling with the rude world, the Son of Man would pitch His tabernacle on a height, if He would establish His seat on the top of the mountain far from the din and strife of men, if He would sit there till suppliants came to *Him* and descend not Himself into the lists of human competition, it seemed to Peter that the new régime would cease to be one of storm and stress, of difficulty and danger, of sorrow and sacrifice, but would become a haven of peace, a home of tranquillity, a place where body and soul could alike find repose. It was his constitutional shrinking from peril that made him wish to remain on the hill.

But, all this time, there was growing up in Simon Peter a new and higher life. Even amid the survivals of his old culture the second stage of his spiritual history had already opened. That second period is one of struggle

—the struggle between the original timidity and a new principle which stimulated to courage. Jacob had begun to wrestle with his angel and, though baffled oft, had refused to let him go. Whence came this element of bravery? It was born of love. There is no mystery about it; you may see the same thing every day. I have seen a soul of extraordinary timidity kindled into a courage which Cæsar might have envied; the fire came from love. One who all through life had shrunk from the slightest hint of danger I have known to rush into a burning house to save her infant from the flames. And yet it does not follow that at this moment the constitutional timidity was dead. The rain may still fall when the sun is shining. Doubtless, where the element of love was absent, this woman would for many a day subside into her old cowardice in the ordinary trifles of life, and to the eye of friends and companions would reveal no spiritual change. None the less the spiritual change would be there, and sooner or later it would leaven the whole nature; for love to one creates love to all, and the courage inspired by my single pure affection will at last become my courage for every danger of my brother-man.

Now, there had come to Peter one great love. He had met with a life which peculiarly dominated him. It dominated him by stilling him, calming him. The very timidity of Peter made Christ to him a special rest; in *that* tabernacle his trembling spirit could repose. And in his devotion to Jesus he had moments of a new experience—courage. At first it came only in thought. He fought battles for Christ in the imagination, stood with Him in vision on the stormy sea, died with Him in the realms of fancy. Let no one say that this profited nothing. All virtue, all vice, begins in thinking. The man who has fought a successful moral battle in his imagination, is already more than half victorious, for it is in imagination that sin looks brightest and virtue seems most hard to win. He may fail betimes in the actual struggle; fancy may drop her lamp for a moment; he may turn his eyes from

the Christ to the sea and the winds raging
But let him faint not.   Success is coming
The battle in the soul is the real test.   The
victory in fancy has guaranteed the triumph
in fact; and he who has conquered in the spirit
will not long be worsted in the flesh.

There came to Simon Peter such a time of
absolute victory.   There came a time when
the struggle with his angel ceased and when
he glowed in the unclouded sun of Peniel.
The final stage of his spiritual experience is
that of unbroken courage.   Timidity vanishes
altogether, and in its room there comes a
calm and habitual fearlessness—not the spasmodic burst of confidence which marked his
earliest days, but a fixed and abiding bravery
pervading all his life and directing all his
way.

How do we know that this was the final
stage of Simon Peter?   Because we have in
our possession a letter written in his mature
life which embodies precisely this spirit.   I
think the letters of the New Testament have
each a special characteristic, a quality which

distinguishes them from beginning to end. The Epistle to the Romans has the quality of reasoning. The Epistle to the Galatians is a letter of self-defence. The Epistle to the Ephesians is a eulogy on Christ's imperialism. The Epistle to the Philippians is in praise of Christian sacrifice. The Epistles to Timothy are a note of exhortation. The Epistles of John are calls to brotherhood. The Epistle of James is a plea for practical religion. What is the Epistle of Peter?—I mean his first, or more undisputed, epistle. What is its characteristic? Can we put our hand upon any chord which pervades all its utterances? I think we can. To my mind there is one theme which runs through this letter as clearly as an air runs through the variations in a piece of music. That theme is courage. Peter has taken for his subject the counterpart of his former self. More than any document of the New Testament this letter is the Epistle of Courage. Other things are accidental; this is its essence, its glory, its crown. In every note, in every bar, in every cadence, we find the

man stepping over his dead self and revealing
the newness of life; the Peter on the top of
the wave looks down upon the Peter sinking
in the depths and cries, 'You were wrong!'

The very first key struck is one of reversal,
'Blessed be God, who has begotten us unto a
lively hope'—a hope pervading the *life*—not
coming periodically in fits and starts, but
taking up its abode within the soul. Listen
again!—'We are redeemed by the precious
blood of Christ as of a lamb without blemish
and without spot.' Where is now the rebuke,
'Be it far from Thee, Lord; this shall not be
unto Thee'!—the thing from which he recoiled
has become 'precious.' Again—'The God of
all grace, after ye have suffered awhile, make
you perfect, stablish, strengthen, settle you.'
What a comment on his own experience! To
be no longer spasmodic, fitful, wayward, but
'stablished,' 'settled'—it was the realisation
of all his wants, and therefore it seemed to
him the crown of all perfection. And then,
notice the boldness of the wish that we should
not be made perfect till after we have 'suffered

awhile'! What a note of autobiography is here! Where is now the call for the three tabernacles that he might be free from the troubles of the plain! To him in his retrospect these troubles have become the glorious things. It is the '*trial* of faith' which he declares to be 'more precious than gold.' In looking back he has such a reverence for the crosses of his life that he would not value perfection without them. The suffering is to him part of the privilege—'Count it all joy!' he cries. He claims the cloud as essential to the clearness, the night as instrumental to the noon. The evening and not the morning is Peter's golden hour. The morning was leaden and grey; the evening is light and glorious. The morning made faint with fear; the evening makes strong with sanguineness. The morning saw his spirit crouch in a coward's lair; the evening leads him forth to dwell in the path of danger. The motto of his maturity is this: 'Forasmuch as Christ has suffered in the flesh, arm yourselves also with the same mind.'

I THANK Thee, O Lord, that there is waiting for each of us a courage in reserve.
This man when he started was quite unfit for
the work that lay before him; he had not
nerve to face life's storm. But it all came—
came with the day and with the hour; it was
reserved in heaven till the crisis moment. I
too, Lord, am unfit for the struggle of life; if I
attempt to walk upon its sea I shall inevitably
sink and perish. I have not the courage to
contemplate the winds and the waves; I am
tempted to fly to the mountain and build a
tabernacle there. But in the light of this
man's experience I will not. What know I
but that my courage may be sleeping beside
the sea, waiting till I come up and claim it!
What know I but that my treasure may be hid
in the very field which seems so desolate and
lonely! Hast Thou not said even of Thyself,
'My hour is not yet come'! I may bear a
cross on Friday which I could not have borne
on the past Monday. If I cannot bear it on
Monday shall I say to my soul, 'Flee as a bird
to your mountain'! Nay, my Christ, for there

may be potent powers of courage sleeping in the folds of Friday. There are angels in the wilderness who only show themselves in the fasting hour. There are angels in Gethsemane who only reveal themselves amid my crying and tears. Shall I wait for the breaking of the cloud before I face the rain! Nay, for my chariot may be *in* the cloud. I shall come without strength to the storm; I shall go without weapons to the wilderness; I shall repair without guarantee to the Garden; I shall journey without courage to the Cross. My shining will come with the shadow; my power will wake with the pain; my courage will rise with the conflict; my fortitude will dawn with the fire; my nerve will be strengthened with the need; my resource will be ready with the rain-cloud; my boldness will be born with the breeze. I shall walk with Thee by faith till the fulness of the time.

6

Nicodemus the Instructed

I AM glad that among the figures of the New
Testament Gallery there is a place assigned
to the student. Great as is our satisfaction
to see an acknowledgment of life's practical
callings, there would, I think, have been an
omission if there had been no portrayal of
the intellectual struggles of the soul. There
is such a portrayal. It appears in the portrait of Nicodemus. He is distinctively the
man of study—the man of the night-lamp.
I do not mean that he represents exclusively
the life of the *university*. The student is
limited to no calling. He may be a fisherman
like Peter or a tax-gatherer like Matthew or
a tentmaker like Paul. Student life is not a
profession; it is a state of mind. There are
very few of us who have not moments of the

night-lamp—times when we sit down and ponder on the mysteries by which we are surrounded. Even the foolish virgins have their lamps—seasons when the seriousness of life breaks through the crust of frivolity and makes them ask the questions which are habitual to the wise. The satisfactory thing about the portraying of Nicodemus is not that it recognises a particular profession, but that it recognises a secret moment of every human heart. It lifts the veil from the innermost life of all men and women, and gives us a glimpse into that sacred shrine which, after all, is the noblest part of man.

In this picture of Nicodemus there are exhibited three phases of the student mind; one of them is good, the other two need correction. We glance at each of these. We begin with that which I have called good. It is the tendency expressed in the saying that Nicodemus 'came to Jesus by night.' I am aware this is commonly recorded to his blame; it is attributed to cowardice. I do not think this is the idea. I think the idea is, he was

so eager that he could not wait till the morning. And I feel sure that the Fourth Evangelist has made the historical fact a grand
symbol both of the man Nicodemus and of
the student life in general. Nicodemus waits
not for light to illumine his way. He comes
in a thick fog — groping, stumbling. The
portrait, in evident support of the metaphor,
introduces him in an attitude of deplorable
ignorance; he has come to Christ, lighted by
a single star. And in this the picture sym-
bolises the initial stage of all inquiry. To
every form of truth the student must come by
night ; he must accept evidence which is less
than demonstration. People talk as if Christianity were in this an exceptional thing ; they
see in its demand for faith an ignoring of the
claims of science. But every scientific theory
makes the same demand. When Darwin
ventilated the doctrine of Evolution, he did
not say it had been proved. What he did say
in effect was this : ' I have found a key which
can unlock many of the doors of this universe.
It is perhaps the key which is meant to un-

lock *all* the doors. I will try. Encouraged by the cases I have established, I shall start by an act of faith. I shall assume that this is the one key to the kingdom of Nature. I shall apply it to the many locks as I have applied it to the few. It may become Aladdin's lamp to me—may open the secrets of creation and unbar the gates of mystery. I shall not wait to exhaust the facts before I form the theory ; I shall begin with the theory and try if it will fit the facts. I shall be content to approach the Temple of Nature with only a night-lamp in my hand ; I shall not linger for the dawn.'

And this is the true source of all discovery in every department of life. Take life itself. With what a very small amount of light we set out to face the world ! We come to it with certain theories in our mind—some gathered from stray testimonies, some derived from the reading of romances. And yet with this slender equipment we go forth into the dark, not only without trembling, but full of the most ardent hope—hope which in the large majority of cases becomes the very key which opens to us the door. But it is in the sphere of knowledge that the principle is most conspicuously, most trenchantly true, and specially in that sphere which we call the knowledge of God. To a mind encompassed with doubts of a Divine Presence in the world I would say: 'Follow the method which originated the doctrine of Evolution. Start with God as a working hypothesis. Do not search for Him in the universe, but search the universe through *Him*. Begin by assuming Him. Say, I have found in Him a key which fits several locks; I want to try it on the other locks. Let your coming be by night— the night of faith. Do not wait till the shadows have cleared away and the unclouded Divine glory is revealed. Approach the universe with a theory—the theory that there is a God. Try the doors with that theory and see if they will open. You will be surprised at your success. You will have as many trophies as the doctrine of Evolution—nay, this theory will explain Evolution itself and make it intelligible to all men.' There is no attitude of mind so seemly in the student, there is no search for knowledge at once so scientific and so reverent, as that which permits faith to precede full enlightenment—which allows man to come by night.

This brings me to the second phase to which the mind of the student is subject. I mean the tendency to sink his own individuality in the life of the race, or what he calls the spirit of the age. This appears very prominently in the case of Nicodemus. Other men when they come into the presence of Jesus address Him as individual suppliants; they say, ' Have mercy upon *me* !' But this man enters into Christ's presence with quite a unique mode of address. He accosts Him as if he were speaking in the name of a corporation, as if he had been deputed to carry a request from a public body—' Master, *we* know that Thou art a teacher come from God.' Here again the popular view is that he is influenced by fear—the wish not to commit himself to a personal opinion regarding Christ. My own

view is that he is influenced purely by pride—
the pride characteristic of the inquirer. One
of the deepest desires of every student is to
be thought a child of his age—up to date, as
the phrase goes. It is a great mistake to
think that the tendency of intellectual youth
is personal independence. Its tendency is
the opposite—the identifying of personal
opinion with the view current among the
highest minds. To obtain the reputation of
this identity, to be called a true son of the
time, the inquirer is content to sacrifice origi-
nality. He delights to repeat the opinions of
the scientific, to quote their names, to air their
views; he begins all things with the formula,
' *We* know.'

Now, this is the position in which I would
place Nicodemus. However ignorant he himself was, he belonged to a guild which was
regarded as the repository of Jewish learning.
With the opinions of that guild he was eager
to identify himself. He did not wish to be
thought peculiar, eccentric. He had no desire
that his coming to Christ should be interpreted

as a mental aberration. He was eager to make it clear that he was saying nothing which the Pharisaic party might not thoroughly endorse. His address is virtually a proposal of terms—a statement of the conditions on which he and his countrymen would be willing to accept Jesus.

You will observe, Jesus resents this corporate mode of address on the part of Nicodemus. I used to wonder why, midway in His speech, He addresses Nicodemus as if he were, not one man, but a whole company of men—says 'ye' instead of 'thou.' But the reason has become clear. Nicodemus has spoken to Jesus as if he were a collective body of men; Jesus *answers* him as if he were a collective body of men. More striking still is the fact that in His answer Jesus *also* assumes a collective capacity: 'Verily, verily I say unto thee, *We* speak what *we* do know and testify what *we* have seen, and ye receive not *our* witness.' It is the only instance I know in the whole New Testament in which our Lord speaks of Himself in the plural number. He says on one occasion, 'If a man love *Me*, My Father will love *him*, and We shall come and take up our abode with him'; but He is there speaking of *two*—Himself and His Father. Here He speaks in His own person, but He uses the editorial 'we.' Can any man fail to see why! It is a fine piece of repartee. Nicodemus has identified himself with his comrades; Christ identifies Himself with His followers. Nicodemus has appealed to the spirit of an earthly age; Christ appeals to the spirit of the ages in heaven, to the mode of thinking which prevails in the upper sanctuary, to the fashion of a world which will *not* pass away.

And let us remember that Christ has here put His hand upon a real weakness of Nicodemus and those whom he represents. For this original tendency of student life is one which needs to be corrected. Specially does it need to be corrected in the religious sphere—the sphere of Nicodemus. The man engaged in a study of God must beware, above all things, of losing himself in the crowd. To him at that moment there is opening a stage of tremendous solemnity— the sense of individual responsibility. In the presence of that thought he should see the whole multitude go out and leave him, alone. The spirit of the age should count for nothing, except so far as it corroborates his own. At that moment, and for that moment, he should feel himself the only man in the world, standing before the most august of all problems, and bound to give an answer from the depths of his own soul. Nicodemus was confronting one who had come to reveal this fact of individual responsibility. Nicodemus himself had belonged to another régime. The adherents of the Jewish faith had uniformly merged the individual in the race. The man only existed for the sake of the nation. It was to *her* that the promises were addressed; it was to her that the warnings were offered. The motto of every son of Israel was, ' My life is my country.' In the interest of that country he was to lose himself, in the fate of that country he was to sink himself. The

personal life was to be absorbed in the
patriotic ; the individual being was to be
blended with the existence of the common-
wealth. Judaism was essentially a national
religion—the man worshipped as a part of
the nation. There was some excuse for
Nicodemus saying, ' *We* know.' But Jesus
was to introduce a new régime. He was to
tell the world that in matters of faith every
man was to God a kingdom. He was to
proclaim that the individual and not the
nation was now to bulk largest in his sight.
He was to proclaim that the Jewish nation
would pass away, but that the man would
endure for ever. He was to proclaim that the
individual in his hour of religious contemplation ought to separate himself sharply from
his environment. He was to bid him enter
into his silent room and shut the door and
pray to his Father in secret—as if in all the
universe there were none other than they two.
The spirit of the age was to be forgotten.
His fellow-men were to be remembered in his
sympathy, but were to have no influence on

his example. He was to feel himself alone—alone with the great problem of eternity, alone with the presence of God.

Nicodemus learned in this interview with Jesus the value of an individual soul, the necessity that it should be lifted into a higher life and born into a world which was independent of Jewish heredity. How do we know that he learned it? Because we have a record on the subject. This man appears before us at a later date and reveals himself in a new attitude. In the interval the atmosphere has changed. Jesus is no longer the object of a kindly and somewhat contemptuous patronage on the part of the Sanhedrin. That august body has been stirred with fear. The movement which at first seemed capable of being incorporated within its own boundaries has flashed out in deadly and irreconcilable antagonism; and the Jewish Assembly, which yesterday was ready to propose terms of union, is to-day animated by only one desire—to crush and annihilate the rising system. The Sanhedrin

is eager to arrest Jesus. It had the pene-
tration to perceive what many professing
Christians have not perceived — that Christianity is Christ, and that to strike at
Christianity you must strike at Christ. It
knew well that the whole force of the movement centred in one man, and that to slay
the one man was to destroy the entire army.
Accordingly, this supreme court resolves to
lay hands on Jesus. But there is one dissent-
ing voice—the voice of Nicodemus. It is the
last voice we should have expected. We are
disposed to say, ' Is this the man who a little
while ago was eager to sink himself in the
spirit of the age!' He now stands forth
opposed to the age—stands out as a solitary
individual breasting the waves of a crowd, and
cries with fearless love of justice, 'Does our
law judge any man before it hears him!' We
marvel at the spectacle. It is not that we see
a growing stature—we expect time to bring
that. It is that we witness a transformation.
Nicodemus has changed his weakness into
a strength. He has become strong in the

very point in which he was defective. On the night in which he stood before Jesus he was unwilling to be alone; on the day in which he stands before the Sanhedrin he is unwilling to be in company. He asserts the right of his own individual soul. He is a fine example of the difference between what is called nature and what is called grace. Nature can improve a man; grace transforms him.

I come now to the third tendency in the life of the inquirer. It is the pride of reason. As applied to Christianity it takes the form of trying to prove Christ from the outside—by something not connected with His nature. We see this with Nicodemus. He says, 'We know that Thou art a teacher come from God, for no man can do these miracles that Thou doest except God be with him.' The answer of Christ is striking and graphic—'Verily verily, I say unto thee, Except a man be born again he cannot see the kingdom of God.' The words, as I take it, are strongly anti-thetical. Our Lord says: 'Nicodemus, you claim to have arrived at *knowledge*. A man

makes a great profession when he says, I
know. There is something which must come
before knowledge, and that is sight. Unless a
man is born with a special faculty, he cannot
even *see* my kingdom—much less understand
it. You cannot reach the sense of my power
by a ladder of demonstration—though you
should mount for ages and ages. But you
may reach it in a moment, in the twinkling
of an eye, if only you can find the wings of
my spirit. If it come to you at all it must
come in a flash, in a thrill of intuition, in
a glance of the soul. It must be *seen*, not
proved ; and the man who sees it gives evidence that he has been born into a world
with larger powers than are at the command
of earth.'

We may illustrate the position of Nicodemus
by one coming to an artist and saying, 'I
know that the city of Edinburgh is beautiful,
because, if otherwise, every one would not
have agreed to call it so.' What would the
artist reply ? Would he not say : 'My friend,
your testimony is absolutely valueless. It

adds nothing to the weight of Edinburgh's prestige. To have any value, your testimony must be founded on sight. It must be independent of any other witness. You must be convinced by your own vision—convinced with equal strength though all other witnesses were contrary. You must be able to feel that the beauty of Edinburgh to you needs no vindication, that you would deem it as fair if all the world contemned it, that it shines to you by its own light and holds the evidence of its own glory.'

The words of our Lord to Nicodemus have often been deemed mystical. I see in them neither mysticism nor mystery. Christianity is no exception when it says, ' He who would know me must be born into my spirit.' There is not a study in the world which would not say that. Have you ever asked yourself what is the first requirement for any study? A knowledge of facts? That is very essential, but it is not the earliest thing. A power of acute reasoning? That is also very essential, but it comes into use still later than the facts. There is something behind these, earlier than these, and that is the spirit of the study itself. Before a man can even begin to inquire, he must ask himself, Am I in sympathy with the subject?—that question must precede all investigation of facts and all lines of reasoning. It matters not what the kingdom be, our first step must be made here. Take the kingdom of art. A man might buy all the pictures in a gallery, might commit to memory their various subjects, might learn their date and authorship, might study the lives of their different painters, might even combine the scattered threads of his information into a connected narrative embodying the rational sequence of the artistic history ; but all this would be only the outside. One touch of inward sympathy would make him independent of all these things. He could dispense with historical knowledge. He could dispense with financial expenditure. He could dispense with efforts of memory. He could feed upon a single picture—though he knew not its name, though he knew not its author, though he could not identify any one of its figures. A very small amount of influence from without is sufficient to stimulate the spirit.

Now, the error of Nicodemus was that he sought Christ for something on the outside. He came to Him for what He wore—that was the sting of the position. He was attracted to Christ by His miracles. This was to Christ quite equivalent to saying, 'I love you for the dress you wear.' There lies the reason for the sternness with which He speaks to Nicodemus. If Nicodemus had come and said, 'Master, I cannot believe in your miracles unless I have seen them, but I am already convinced of your Divine beauty,' Jesus would have received him very differently; for the only power He valued was the power of the spirit, and He felt that the power of His spirit was something which flesh and blood could not reveal.

But here again Nicodemus has a magnificent counterpart. We have seen how grandly the previous tendency was reversed, transformed. We have seen how the man who clung to the fashion of his age became the man who could stand to his opinion unbefriended and alone. We are now to see a greater transformation still. This man who at the beginning accepted Christ's miracles and ignored His Divine beauty was able in the end to ignore His miracles and accept His beauty! In the latest recorded scene in which he appears before us he comes in a deeper and darker night than that in which he first sought the Lord. Jesus is dead. All the Messianic hopes seem faded in the dust. The hosannahs are hushed, the palm-leaves are withered, the friends of summer days have made their flight in the winter. It was a time when, if the first view of Nicodemus had been right, God must have deserted Jesus. All power had vanished from Him—even the power to live. There He lay—shorn of His outward beams, denuded of His visible glory, stripped of the robe of earthly royalty! And it was at this moment that Nicodemus came. He came

to do homage to the dead, to embalm the
body of the prostrate Lord. He brought
myrrh and aloes of a hundred-pound weight
—far more than could possibly be used for the
purpose. It was like the woman's alabaster
box—the prodigality of love. And, like the
pouring out of that ointment, it was an
anointing for burial. He recognised Christ's
majesty in death—this man who had begun
with the love of the external! He saw His
glory in the night; he beheld His chariot
in a cloud ; he discerned His kingdom under
the trappings of the grave ! It was a grand
act, worthy to constitute our last glimpse of
the man. It was an act, moreover, which
lends to the picture of Christ's life a strange
poetic consistency. Twice in that picture do
we see the myrrh laid at the unconscious feet
of Jesus ; and both tributes are given by
inquiring minds. The first offering was laid
before the infant by the Persian Magi ; the
second was made to the dead Christ by the
Jewish Nicodemus. To me there is something
beautiful in the thought that, amid all the

selfish approaches to Jesus, amid all the crowds that sought Him only for what He could bestow, there were some who recognised Him in the days of His weakness, and paid their tribute to a sense of inward beauty. The myrrh presented in the manger and the myrrh lavished on Calvary are the truest embalming of the greatness of our Lord.

IT is Thy death that has embalmed Thee, O Christ. Many things have *glorified* Thee; but death has embalmed Thee. The myrrh and the aloes have remained in Thy sepulchre. Nowhere dost Thou live in memory so bright as in the valley of the shadow. In a deeper sense than Nicodemus, we come to Thee 'by night.' Not in Thy miracles art Thou embalmed, but where Thy miracles have ceased. We have seen Thy beauty where the world saw only Thy weakness; Thou hast survived where men thought Thee most unfit. We have brought our crown to Thy discrowned brow; we have put our trust in Thine unsceptred hand. We have kept our spices for Thy grave. We have not scattered them on Hermon where mighty words were spoken; we have not spread them in the wilderness where wondrous bread was broken; we have not left them on the Transfiguration Mount which gave Thee heaven's token. We have passed these by. We have laid the myrrh and aloes upon the altar of Thy sacrifice. We have brought our faith to Thy seeming feebleness, our prayer to Thine apparent powerlessness. We have drawn courage from Thy crucifixion, strength from Thy stripes, wealth from Thy wounds, boldness from Thy blood. We have seen Thy kingdom in the cloud, Thine empire in the embers, Thy power in the unbeating pulse, Thy glory in the graveclothes, Thy victory in the hour of vanquishment, Thy destiny coming from the dust. We pay our tribute to Thy cross. We lay our myrrh and aloes where the old world laid its scorn—upon Thy broken heart; but one who once belonged to that world meets us at the garden gate and cries, 'You have done well.' It is the voice of Nicodemus.

7

Thomas the Convinced

THERE are two classes of minds which habitually stand in the post of outlook—the man of the laurel and the man of the cypress. The first sees the world as rose-coloured. It is all brightness, all beauty, all glory—a scene of splendid possibilities which is waiting to open for him its gates of gold. The second, on the other hand, approaches it with dismay. To him the prospect looks all dark. He is a pessimist previous to experience. He is sure he will never succeed. He is sure the gate will not open when he tries it. He feels that he has nothing to expect from life. He hangs his harp upon a willow, and goes forth to sow in tears.

And each of these has a representative in the New Testament. I think the man of the laurel is the evangelist John. From the very beginning he is optimistic. Even when Christ was on the road to that martyrdom of which He had warned His disciples, John is so sanguine of success that he applies for a place in the coming kingdom. And through life this optimism does not desert him. His very power to stand beside the cross was a power of hope. It was not that he excelled his brother-disciples in the nerve to bear pain. It was rather that to him the spectacle conveyed an impression of less pain—that he saw in it elements of triumph as well as trial, signs of strength along with marks of sacrifice.

But if the man of the laurel is John, the man of the cypress is assuredly Thomas. There are men whose melancholy is the result of their scepticism; Thomas's scepticism is the result of his melancholy. He came to the facts of life with an antecedent prejudice; he uniformly expected from the banquet an inferior menu. It is a great mistake to imagine that the collapse came with the Crucifixion. Strictly speaking, there was no collapse. If

I understand the picture aright, it represents
the figure of a man who could never stand
at his full stature but was always bent towards
the ground. It was not from timidity. He
was a courageous man, ready to do and dare
anything even when he was most downcast.
It was not from a mean nature. He was a
man of the noblest spirit — capable of the
most heroic deeds of sacrifice. That which
gave him a crouching attitude was simply a
constitutional want of hope — a natural inability to take the bright view. It was this
which made him a sceptic. He was indisposed
to give anything a trial. When the disciples
assembled at their first spiritual séance in the
hope of getting a vision of their risen Lord,
he refused to attend;[1] when told that a vision
had been given, he refused to believe it. It
was too good news to be true. He would
have believed the story of an earthquake or
a pestilence or a shipwreck; but he could not

[1] I think the same religious hopelessness would keep him
from attending the meeting for silent individual prayer in
Gethsemane; I do not believe he was one of those who fled
that night.

credit the earth with the power to witness a scene of glory.

Now, the question which arises is this, Why is Thomas so leniently treated? He demands as an evidence of the risen Christ that very kind of proof which the Pharisees had demanded as an evidence of the *Divine* Christ— a physical sign. We know how Christ treated the Pharisaic demand, how He had said, 'An evil and adulterous generation seeketh after a sign, and there shall no sign be given unto it.' Is it thus that our Lord meets Thomas? On the contrary, He grants his request—not perhaps without reproach, but certainly without loss of tenderness; He bids him put forth his hand and *touch* the material sign—the print of the nails. There must have been something in Thomas which won upon Christ, which made the request in his case comparatively harmless. What was it? It is a question well worthy of our consideration. We are familiar with the saying that circumstances alter cases; it is equally true that persons alter cases. The boon of a physical sign denied to the Jewish nation is granted to a Jewish individual. There must have been something in that individual which to the eye of the Master changed the complexion of the case and rendered it possible to relax the rigidness of the rule.

And a moment's reflection will convince us that in the picture of Thomas we have a specimen quite unique in the male section of Christ's first hearers—a figure which must have been unique even to Jesus Himself. For consider, the natural melancholy of this man made his approach to Christ an unselfish one. He expected nothing from the world— nothing from a world even under the auspices of Christ. Yet he *came* to Christ—spite of this absence of physical expectation. Whatever drew him to the Master, it could have been nothing external. Here was something fresh and new. All around Him Christ saw men who came on the chance of a physical glory. The sign they asked was not so much a sign of Christ as a sign of their own felicity. Even the circle of the apostolic band was pervaded by the hope of a physical glory. With some it took the form of Messianic conquest; with others, like Simon Peter, it assumed the aspect of an earthly Paradise far from the din of men. But whatever form it took, it had always the same essence—outward reward. The Christ was measured by His power to change the present order of physical things—to place two ignorant fishermen at the right hand of heaven, to bid the stones be turned into bread, to change earth's water into plenteous wine, and expand the few loaves into food for the million.

But here is a man who approaches Jesus in a totally different attitude. He was a man of the cypress—a man to whom the world did not present possibilities. I do not say it did not present attractions; but where attractions are believed to be beyond our reach they have no motive power. It is a proverbial saying that an infant cries for the moon. But the infant cries for the moon because it believes that luminary to be within its reach; if it had a contrary belief, we are absolutely safe in stating that it would not cry. All aspiration is born of hope. If I believe an object to be beyond the stretch of my arm, I do not stretch my arm towards it. It is equally true with the things of the heart. I do not make an effort to attain that which I know to be entirely above me; desire, in such cases, is paralysed on the threshold. And such I conceive to be the case of Thomas. He looked at the world from under his cypress-tree, and he pronounced it an impossible world—a world whose gates of promotion and whose doors of promise were not for him. He had too keen a sense of life's difficulties to be impelled by any worldly hope in Christ, and therefore he never could have joined Christ for any such motive. Yet he did join Him. He threw in his lot with Jesus and accompanied His train. Why? So must have asked the Son of Man Himself; and the answer His mind gave must have been refreshing in the extreme. Amid the many who came to Him for His sur-

roundings, here was one who came to Him
for Himself. Christ beheld in Thomas a
devotion to His *person*. Had he recognised in
the Master some of his own cypress leaves—
something which prevented Him from having
fulness of joy? I cannot tell; but I know
that the man of depression drew close to
the Man of Sorrows, and I feel that the bond
between them was stronger than any material
chain.

In this portrait of Thomas I think there are
revealed two things of great significance. We
see a Christian love in the absence of a Christian creed; and we see what is more remarkable still—a Christian *faith* in the absence of
a Christian creed. Let us look at each of
these separately.

And first. Let us take one central incident
in the portraiture of Thomas. Perhaps if the
question were asked, What is the most central
incident in the portraiture of Thomas? the
majority would answer, ' The touching of the
nail-prints.' That is not my opinion. I think
the circumstance which most broadly marks

the character of Thomas is his attitude towards
Jesus on hearing of the death of Lazarus.
Let us review the facts for a moment.

There has been a commotion in the streets
of Jerusalem. The transition of Jesus from
the work of a reformer to the work of a
theologian has produced also a transition in
the feelings of the multitude. They pass at a
bound from applause to reprobation. Goaded
by the suggestion of heresy in His teaching,
they assail Him with stones. The majesty of
Christ's presence saves Him—paralyses the
directness of their aim. Evading the fury of
the populace, He retires into a secluded place,
and for some time is visible only to His disciples. At last, to this desert spot come
tidings of the death of Lazarus. Then Jesus
resolves to return. The disciples are startled
—on His account and their own. They are
very unwilling to come into the vicinity of a
place which had been so fraught with fear, so
full of danger. Jesus, for His part, is determined. He says, 'I go.' He does not ask
any one to accompany Him; He simply ex-

presses His personal resolve. Then through the silence one man speaks out for the company—'Let us also go, that we may die with Him!' It is the voice of Thomas.

Now, I say that this utterance of Thomas reveals at one and the same moment the deepest scepticism and the highest love. The scepticism does not lie in his expectation of Christ's death. That was the very thing which Christ *wished* His disciples to expect, nay, to build their hopes upon. But the scepticism of Thomas comes out in the belief that the death of Jesus would be the death of His kingdom. 'Let us go, that we may die with Him.' The man who uttered these words had, at the time when he uttered them, no hope of Christ's resurrection. No man would propose to die with another if he expected to see him again in a few hours. Thomas, at that moment, had given up all intellectual belief. He saw no chance for Jesus. He did not believe in His physical power. He had made up his mind that the forces of the outer world would be too strong for Him, would crush Him. The penitent said to the dying Lord, 'Remember me when Thou comest in Thy kingdom.' Thomas could not say that; he saw no kingdom beyond the death; he could only cry, 'Let me die with Him!'

But what a cry was that! It was the voice of a boundless love. The natural sequence to the view held by Thomas would have been, 'The game is lost; save yourselves who can!' The average man would have said, 'Our Master is bent on a course which must inevitably end in the ruin of His cause; it now becomes imperative that we should provide for ourselves.' Thomas says, on the contrary, 'It now becomes imperative that I should *share* His ruin—die with Him.' It is what I would call the logic of love—a kind of reasoning which on any other ground would be deemed absurd. It never occurred to Thomas that there could be a possibility of separation between his interests and the interests of his Master. In his mind they were one. He would have been glad to have shared in His good fortune had good fortune been His lot; but since the cypress and not the laurel had been His, the only remaining consolation was the possibility of being overtaken by the same storm and crushed in the same ruin. I know not in all the opening life of the apostolic band where to look for such a form of love. To find it in the primitive Gospel I must go out of that band. To meet with a perfect analogy I must go to those women who followed Jesus from the obscurity of Galilee to the obsequies of the grave. I think they were animated by the love that dwelt within the heart of Thomas— the love which could exist even amid the belief that Christ had no outward sun. I think these women *believed* that Christ had no outward sun. They came to the sepulchre; but it was not because they looked for His resurrection; it was to anoint His body with the spices. Their whole solicitude was for the preservation of the body; 'They have taken away my Lord,' cries one of them, 'and I know not where they have laid Him!' They never would have brought the spices if they had expected a resurrection. Why anoint a body for the grave which the grave in a few hours was to yield up to life and liberty! The bringing of the spices was the highest proof of their shattered creed, and it was at the same moment the strongest evidence of their deathless love. They had taken up at the last the uncrowned Christ whom they had accepted at the beginning, and they had lavished upon Him all the treasure of their hearts. To these feminine souls Thomas was more allied than to any of the first apostles in their first days. He was drawn to the Master by something which the world could neither give nor take away; he had not expected the crown and he was not repelled by the cross.

But this same fact has a second aspect. It not only reveals a Christian *love* existing in the absence of a creed, but a Christian faith existing in the absence of a creed. For, let us understand distinctly what that was for which Thomas was prepared to die. It was an ideal. Paul says there is a faith which worketh by love. The love of Thomas reveals such a faith. What he proposed to die for was really a belief—the belief that death with Jesus was better than life without Him. I would call this a dogma of love as distinguished from a dogma of knowledge. It was an article of faith prescribed by the heart and enshrined in the book of the affections. Thousands of martyrs have died for their faith in Jesus; Thomas was willing to do so too. What is the difference between the faith of Thomas and the faith of the martyrs? It is this: The martyrs saw the sacrifice from under the laurel; Thomas contemplated it from beneath the cypress. The martyrs had their eye upon the rainbow; Thomas looked upon the cloud. The martyrs were convinced, not only of Christ's spiritual beauty, but of His physical power; Thomas was satisfied only of the former. The martyrs beheld an eternity beyond; Thomas did not. Hence the martyrs really said, 'Let us die *for* Him'; Thomas exclaimed, 'Let us die *with* Him.' It is the difference between optimism and pessimism; but it is not a difference in the intensity of faith. When I say, 'I believe in that man,'

I express my confidence in the man himself
—confidence in his honour, in his uprightness,
in his integrity of character. If I should be
obliged to entertain dark views about his
worldly prospects, this will sadden me, but it
will in no wise shake my faith. My faith was
not in his worldly prospects, but in himself—
in my ideal of the man ; and that ideal will
remain unbroken, undimmed, unaltered, by
any contingency that can befall his fortunes.

But behind this cry of Thomas there is
something more—something which gives his
faith an aspect higher than he himself knew.
For, what was this determination to die with
Jesus ? It was really an unconscious act of
homage to the majesty of a human soul. He
was declaring, not by word but by deed, that
mind is greater than matter, nay, that a single
mind can to him outweigh all the material
glories of the universe—its suns and its systems, its silver and its gold. The man whose
deed could say that, was very near the hope
of immortality. He might call himself an
agnostic, an unbeliever, a man without a

creed; but the mental act of sacrifice to the majesty of mind proclaimed him not far from the vision of eternal life. I do not wonder that Jesus offered him an aid to the belief in resurrection. It was worth while to help such a soul. He was nearer to the belief in resurrection than many who professed it. He had not seen the city of gold; but he had seen the transcendent beauty of the human soul. To have the vision of such a beauty is to be more than half-way to the happy land of Beulah. There are a greater number in the world like Thomas than the world dreams of. There are those whom we call secularists, nay, who call themselves so. They say, 'Never mind looking beyond the skies; let us attend to the wants of our brother-man; let us surrender our lives to the life of humanity!' And many of these labour in that cause with great success. But why? It is because, like Thomas, they think man more worth serving than matter. There is more in their heart than in their catechism. Their catechism says, 'Do not look beyond the earth '; but their eye has in an unconscious moment already looked beyond and seen that humanity is more than common clay.   Living philanthropy is latent faith.

I have been endeavouring to account for the problem involved in that wonderful episode of the Picture where Thomas is represented as asking a special sign that Christ has risen— ' Except I shall see in His hands the print of the nails, and thrust my hand into His side, I will not believe.'   The problem lies in the fact that the request is granted—that Christ in the case of Thomas departs from His usual practice of discouraging speculative curiosity. But where we err is in attributing that spirit to Thomas.   I have heard Thomas described again and again as a speculative mind—a mind seeking to dive into the secrets of the future.   A more unfair view of his posi- tion is not to be conceived.   Perhaps he was the least speculative of all the apostles, and for the very reason that he was the least hopeful.   Speculation is inspired by hope.   It was hope that made Peter see his vision at

Joppa. It was hope that gave John his vision at Patmos. It was hope that opened to Paul a glimpse of the highest heaven. But Thomas was not a man of hope; he was a man of despair. Curiosity was no part of his nature. His cry for a sign of the risen Christ was not really a cry for the resurrection; the present life had not been so bright to him as to make him interested in another. But what he *was* interested in was the survival of his Lord Himself. What cried out for satisfaction was not his curiosity but his love. The sign he asked was a sign that his Master was alive —a sign that he could meet Him again, speak to Him again, commune with Him again. Thomas had no wish to lift the curtain of eternity. He was content to remain in *ignorance* of what 'the angels desire to *look into*.' All he wanted was to be convinced that his Lord was in the land of the living by the touch of a vanished hand and the sound of a voice that had been still.

And Christ granted him that conviction. 'Reach hither thy finger,' He says, 'and behold My hands, and thrust thy hand into My side, and be not faithless but believing'; and with a great cry love recognises its object and clasps its restored treasure. But even in his moment of transport Thomas receives an intimation that the sign which he asked was not the best thing—'Because thou hast seen, thou hast believed; blessed are they that have not seen and yet have believed.' What does Christ mean by these words? It is worth while asking, for they express the reason of His habitual unwillingness to reveal Himself by material signs. Are we to understand that it is a more blessed thing to believe on slender evidence than on grounds of assured conviction? This is, I think, the common interpretation. The value of faith is supposed to lie in its want of credentials. One of the Church fathers says, 'I believe, because it is impossible.' It reminds one of the familiar story of a little girl in a Sunday-school who, when asked to define 'faith,' wrote this answer—'It is the power to believe something which you know to be false.' But our Lord's view here is just the opposite of this. When He says, 'Blessed are they that have not seen and yet have believed,' He means that they are blessed because their faith rests on higher evidence—the evidence not of the sense but of the soul. The writer of the Acts says that Christ burst the bands of death because it was not possible death should hold Him. This is what I call unseen evidence—his Christ was not immortal because He rose from the grave; He rose from the grave because He was immortal. If the rising had taken place unknown to any human soul, it would not have altered this man's opinion. Christ and death were to him two irreconcilable quantities; he could not think of them together. His formula would be, not 'the Resurrection proves Christ,' but 'Christ proves the Resurrection.' That is a faith which Christ pronounces, which we must pronounce, blessed. To feel that the life of Jesus is its own witness, that the purity of His heart is bound to see the King in His beauty, that the self-surrender of His spirit ensures Him the kingdom of heaven, that His mourning for sin demands in the hereafter a compensating comfort, that His meekness merits a future inheritance, that His hunger and thirst after man's righteousness has a claim to be filled 'in the sweet by and by' —this is a faith which rests upon a rock impregnable, and compared to whose blessedness the sight of material wonders is poor indeed.

LORD, there are times in which my experience is the experience of Thomas. There are days when I hear not the bells of Easter Morn. I tread the road to Emmaus, and I meet not the risen Christ. I call to the five hundred brethren, and they answer not. I stand on the mountain of Galilee, and there comes no voice amid the breezes. I sail on Gennesaret's lake, and I see no vision. I frequent the upper room, and get no hint of His presence. My faith cannot walk by sight in hours like these. What shall I do at such times, O Lord! Hast Thou a remedy

for the loss of light ?   Yes, my Father.   Thou
hast a gate where faith can enter without
seeing where it goes ; its name is Love.   Lead
me by that gate when my eye is dim !   When
I cannot follow Him to Olivet, let me worship
Him on Calvary !   When betimes I lose sight
of His risen form, do not shut me out from
the bearing of His name !   In the days when
immortal hope is dim, make room in my
heart for immortal memory !   If I cannot
soar with Him into heaven, let me at least
go back to finish His work on earth !   Let
me gather the fragments of the cross which
remain on the Dolorous Way !   Let me dis-
tribute of the twelve baskets which were not
served in the wilderness !   Let me take up
His burden at the spot where He was too
faint to carry it !   Let me mourn with the
Marthas whose Lazarus I cannot raise !   Let
me pray with the paralytics whose weakness
I cannot cure !   Let me sing to the sightless
whose eyes I cannot open !   Let me lend to
the lepers the touch of a brother's hand !   Let
me find for the fallen a chance to renew their

days! Then shall my evidence come back—brighter, stronger. Then shall my Easter Morn shine again through the clouds of night. Then shall I know the meaning of these words: 'Blessed are they that have not seen, and yet have believed.'

8

Philip the Disillusioned

A COLOURLESS face may have very strong features. There are faces in the New Testament Gallery whose colourlessness repels us. We wonder how they have found their way into such an august company. To drop the metaphor, their lives seem devoid of incident. Their names occur but once or twice on the Sacred Page, and in a connection apparently so trivial as to leave nothing worth transmitting. But as we look longer and closer, we change our mind. We feel as if suddenly a microscope had been put into our hand. The seeming trifle assumes magnitude, the passing reference becomes big with suggestion, the commonplace statement is found to be full of significance; and the man who at first appeared a mere cipher takes his place among the leading men of the Gallery and the representative men of the world.

One of the best instances of this is, I think, to be found in Philip of Bethsaida. The common impression is that we know nothing about him. For a long time I studied his countenance in vain. It seemed expressionless, characterless. No ray flashed from the eye to awaken human interest. The man appeared a lay figure placed in the group merely to fill up a gap. Was there any personality about him—anything worth converting, worth transmitting, worth transforming? At first one was disposed to answer, No. Yet I felt that my impression must be wrong. This man was sought out by Jesus Himself. He was the first who ever heard the Christian command, 'Follow me!' Jesus sought those who were sick — physically, morally, or mentally. His seeking of Philip implied that there was something to remove. I felt that this 'something' must be indicated, and that if I searched long enough I ought to find it. I did search, long and patiently,

and I think I have found it—have discovered
that element in Philip which rendered him
a man requiring the Master's care and representing through all time one section of
mankind.

The question then is, What is, in Philip's
case, the stone which had to be rolled from
the door of the sepulchre, in other words,
what was the original imperfection of his
nature? We have seen the moral impedi-
ments of others—how the Baptist needed
expansion, John self-forgetfulness, Peter
courage, Nathanael robustness, Nicodemus
instruction, Thomas hope. What did Philip
need? Can we put our hand upon *his* barrier?
Can we tell the nature of that moral struggle
which raises his life from insignificance to
interest, and gives him a permanent place
among the great cloud of witnesses?

I think we can. It seems to me that the
moral impediment of Philip was an illusion
about the nature of the religious life. He
thought religion was something above the
common plain. It was too serious a matter

to be concerned in the ordinary duties of the world, too solemn a thing to be brought down to streets and 'openings of the gates.' By all means the duties of the hour should be attended to, but they ought to have their own agencies. Religion should be made to dwell in a higher and purer atmosphere. It should be kept for ecstatic moments in which the world can be forgotten and time can be no more — moments in which the soul is carried right into the presence of its God, and hears things which cannot be spoken amid the duties of the earthly day. At such times the world must drop from a man like Elijah's garment, and all his mundane responsibilities must be overshadowed by another and a higher life.

Why do I think that this was the original view of Philip? From two episodes in his history, both recorded in the Fourth Gospel. Nothing can exceed the apparent difference between these two episodes. The one is at the breaking of bread in the wilderness ; the other occurs at that solemn hour when

Christ in His farewell sermon was raising the thoughts of His disciples to the sources of spiritual peace. The one is in the sphere of the secular; the other is in the region which men call sacred. The one is concerned with the wants of the body; the other is occupied with the needs of the soul. The one is a scene of philanthropy; the other is a scene of piety. In both of these opposite episodes Philip is a prominent figure. And yet I have no hesitation in saying that in each of them he has one and the same attitude. In each of these varied circumstances we find the man subject to the same illusion —the belief that religion is something too high and holy to be identified with the good works of common day. I think this will become evident if we consider the episodes separately.

I begin with the earlier. Jesus has crossed the Sea of Tiberias and has reached its eastern shore. Great crowds are coming in the same direction—some from the scattered ranks of the Baptist, some consisting of the pilgrims

to the Passover at Jerusalem. Both are
naturally drawn to Jesus—the disciples of the
Baptist by a kindred association, the Passover
pilgrims by a spirit of devotion. We should
have thought Jesus would have grasped the
moment as one eminently adapted to the
spread of His doctrines. Strange to say, His
whole interest is bent upon something else.
He thinks entirely of the *physical* wellbeing of
that crowd. They must already be hungry
and faint with their journey. If they are to
interrupt that journey to listen to Him, they
will be more faint and hungry still. Accordingly, Christ's primal care is for their bodies,
their food, their nourishment. He intends
that before all things they shall receive provision for their *temporal* wants. But he is not
content to achieve that; He wishes His disciples to go along with Him, to sympathise
with Him. And so, He starts a problem of
political economy — How shall we procure
food for this multitude ; is there any neigh-
bouring store from which we can buy? It is
Philip that He addresses—probably because

He feels that Philip is the most likely to be surprised at such a human interest on His part. Philip's answer is certainly not sympathetic—' It is impossible; even if you could get two hundred pennyworth of loaves it would not suffice to give a small amount to each; the scheme must be abandoned.'

For this answer Philip has reaped much obloquy. The obloquy is just; but I think it is bestowed on wrong grounds. Philip is blamed for losing faith in the Messianic power of Jesus—a power in which originally he strongly believed. But I do not think this was really his position. This man was no sceptic about the claims of Christ. He had not lost one jot of his faith in the Messianic mission of Jesus. Where he erred was in denying to that Messianic mission a right to be interested in what he called trifles. It is another form of the objection to the blessing pronounced on the little children. The love for children was all right, and the nurture and admonition of children were desirable; but to single them out as a section of Christ's army, to ordain them publicly to a great Messianic work—this was something which seemed incongruous with the Christ. So did the proposal in the wilderness. Benevolence was good and the wants of the poor a legitimate subject of solicitude ; but it was deemed a subject for the economist, for the capitalist, for the citizen. It was surely no part of the province of Messiah Himself! Was it not a thing for His agents, His subordinates! Was not the Messiah's work cosmopolitan—concerned with momentous issues and big with solemn interests! It could never be expected that He should interrupt that work to give personal attention to a trifle of the hour!

I feel sure that this, and not want of faith, was the motive of Philip's answer to Jesus. It was his opinion that Jesus would not think it worth while to manifest His power in a scene so humble. And I believe that in His subsequent act of political economy the design of Jesus was to counteract this impression. The narrative as given by St. John clearly implies that Jesus intended here to make

Himself the subject of a special revelation. But what about Himself did He wish to reveal? Was it the fact that He had power to expand a meagre repast into a great banquet? No; it was the fact that He had the *will* to do so, that He did not deem it beneath His dignity to do so. That was what He wanted the multitude to learn; that was what He wanted Philip to learn; that was what He desired the world of all times to learn. We have still our Philips among us—men of devout faith who yet by their very devotion divide God too much from man. To all such the old narrative carries the eternal moral that the God of the telescope must be the God of the microscope too, and that the Power which guides the Pleiades must be able to direct a sparrow's wing. The later Isaiah says of God, 'He calleth the stars all by name; because He is great in power not one faileth.' The Philips of the world would have inverted the state-ment, would have said, 'Because He is great in power He cannot be expected to take care of individuals.' But the words of the prophet

are held true also by the evolutionist, and
religion has here found an ally in science.
The claim of seeming trifles to be subjects of
Universal Law is one of the greatest lessons
this world has ever received.

I come now to the second episode which
indicates the limitation in the character of
Philip. It occurs in a totally different direction, but it reveals the same tendency. The
scene is that hour between the Passover and
Gethsemane when Jesus delivers His parting
message. It is distinctively a message to the
troubled *heart*. Other messages had been
addressed to different sides of human nature.
Some had been spoken to the troubled body;
they had brought the words of healing. Some
had been spoken to the troubled conscience;
they had breathed the words of pardon. Some
had been spoken to the troubled spirit—
troubled as to where lay its road to duty;
they had pointed, like the Sermon on the
Mount, to a life of sacrifice. But this last
message of our Lord was spoken to the
troubled heart. It was a season of bereave-

ment. The disciples were losing the object
of their dearest love. For the first time perhaps in their lives, their souls were intent on
the problem of immortality. Therefore it is
of immortality that Christ speaks. He tells
them of a life beyond, of a place which He is
about to prepare for them in the mansions of
heaven. He tells them that He is going to
no foreign scene, but to the house of His
Father. He tells them that neither will *they*
find it foreign—that they will be where *He* is,
and so have a sense of home. But Christ's
deep teaching has taught these men to be
critical. They begin to question—they ask
how they are to get there, and where the
region lies. Then Philip makes a bold proposal. He suggests a method by which all
doubts will be lulled to rest. Let Christ give
them a vision of the Father—of the Father
Himself—of the primal source of all being,
without any intermediate veil. You will
observe the thoroughness of the demand. He
wants no manifestation from the stage—Jesus
had given many such. He wants to get

behind the scenes, to get into the greenroom, to know the private counsels which guide the drama of life. He is determined to go to the root of the matter, and the root of the matter is to him the beginning of creation, 'Lord, show us the Father, and it sufficeth.'

Now, there is one respect in which Philip was right. He was right in thinking that our best evidence of immortality comes from the vision of the Father. I cannot understand how any man who has a firm conviction of the fatherhood of God can be sceptical about the immortality of the soul. Remember, I speak of the *fatherhood* of God. I do not think the mere belief in an author of the universe is sufficient to bring the conviction of human immortality. We have seen men like Francis Newman accepting the existence of a Supreme Power and yet refusing their assent to the other doctrine. No man would be entitled to say, 'Show us that there is an unknown power in the universe, and it sufficeth.' But every man is entitled to say, 'Show us the Father, and it sufficeth.' It was not *there* that the fault of Philip lay; Christ's answer virtually admits that he was right. The highest evidence of immortality is the vision of a God who has a relation to the human soul. The very incompleteness of that soul then becomes an argument in its favour. For, in the light of Divine fatherhood, we say, 'God will not leave His structure unfinished; He must have determined to finish it elsewhere.' Tennyson cries, 'Thou art just; Thou wilt not leave me in the dust.' It may seem a bold thing in a matter of this kind to appeal to the justice rather than to the mercy of God. It is worse than bold if God be not our Father. But if God be our Father, His mercy and His justice are one. The yearning of a human soul becomes itself a claim. The aspiration of a human heart becomes itself a right. The cry of a human spirit becomes itself a call for the fulfilment of a promise.

Philip, then, was justified in his view that the shortest road to the hope of immortality is a vision of the Father. But he neutralised his doctrine by taking a long road to that *vision.* Where Philip erred was in the belief that a vision of the Father was best reached by getting away from human contact or, to repeat the old metaphor, by quitting the stage for the greenroom. To him the Divine was something apart from the human; to behold it he must withdraw himself. He must retire from the footlights, from the drapery, from the actors in the scenes of time. He must get behind the scenes. He must seek a moment of ecstasy in which he will be raised above the things of the day and of the dust and ushered into that august Presence which transcends the works of man.

And this is the view of Philip which our Lord combats here. He tells him that the knowledge of the Father is not reached in the way he supposes. He tells him that the love of the Father is learned *on* the stage of time—not behind it, 'He that has seen *Me* hath seen the Father, and how sayest thou then, Show us the Father!' He tells him that it is not where human work is transcended that we get our deepest glimpse of the Divine;

it is precisely where human work is richest—
'The Father that dwelleth in *Me* doeth the
works.' Would Philip believe in Divine fatherhood, let him study human brotherhood. Let
him consider the spirit of Christ as it exists
in the *world*. Let him ponder how through
that spirit man has sacrificed for man, how
love has dared many a cross, how sympathy
has shared many a sorrow, how pity has dried
many a tear, how compassion has healed many
a pain, how benevolence has assuaged many
a hunger. Let him ponder these things, and
he will reach a clearer vision of the fatherhood
of God than if he stood in the forest primeval
in the solitary presence of the Divine.

Such is the burden of Christ's message to
Philip. I have been struck with the fact that
before it became a formal message it was made
a practical training. We read that—some
three years earlier—immediately after Jesus
had called him to join the league of pity, he
brought another man to the league—'Philip
findeth Nathanael.' Why does he rush at
once to secure a companion in his own calling?

We do not wonder when we are told that
Andrew, after his own call, finds his brother
Simon. These *were* brothers, and it was
inevitable that either adversely or favourably
the act of the one should influence the other.
But Philip and Nathanael were not brothers;
to find the latter required a seeking on the
part of the former. Why does Philip hasten
to implant in the heart of another a conviction
at which he himself had only arrived yesterday? I believe the answer to be that he was
told to do so. I think that the moment he
gave his allegiance to Jesus, Jesus said to him,
' Find Me an additional man.' And I believe
the reason of this request was not the helping
of Jesus but the helping of Philip. Jesus
might have called Nathanael by a telepathic
message; but Philip would thereby have lost
an element in his education. If Philip was
the man we have found him to be—with a
tendency to underrate the practical, there
could be no better introduction to his Christian
training than to give him practical work. He
ought not to be allowed to go home and

dream of twelve legions of angels. Let him
look to the help of his brother-man, nay, let
him make an effort to initiate that help. Let
him use his human judgment. Let him find
a man himself—one whom he believes to be
fitted for the great work of inaugurating the
future kingdom. All education should be
directed to the weak point of a nature. If
you see one like Paul whose life has been
entirely occupied with the practical, send him
into Arabia—seclude him for a time that he
may meditate. If, on the other hand, you see
one like Philip disposed to look for God in
things behind the scenes, send him into the
practical world—let him find an additional
man.

As a further contribution to this training,
Philip, in the latest days of Christ's ministry, is
made the instrument of a wondrously practical work quite on the lines of his search for
Nathanael. If you or I were suddenly asked
the question, Which of the Christian disciples
brought the earliest help to the Gentiles? I do
not think we should immediately hit the answer.

We should probably say 'Paul' or 'Peter' or
'Stephen.' But in truth there was one before
any of these—it was Philip. After our Lord
Himself, the first who spoke a word to the
Gentiles was this obscure man of Bethsaida.
Before Peter had called Cornelius, before
Stephen had lifted his voice, before Paul had
raised his banner, Philip had brought a Gentile
band into the presence of Jesus. True, they
were the descendants of Jews ;[1] but they had
been born in a foreign land, bred in a foreign
culture, trained in foreign ideas. They had
become Greeks in nationality, Greeks in education, Greeks in taste, Greeks in manner. But
they had heard of the fame of Jesus, and they
longed to see Him. Their pride in the old
ancestry was not dead. They were glad that
where their fathers' homes had been, there
had risen a great light. How were they to
gaze upon that light? The Jews would now
despise them, count them aliens. Yet they

---

[1] I have taken this view instead of the prevalent one which
makes these men pure Greeks ; I do not think the latter view
sufficiently accounts for their interest in Jesus.

would try. The Passover Feast was coming on; they would go up to Jerusalem; perchance some one might show them the new star. They come; and they are gladdened by a discovery. Among the names of Christ's inner circle they hear of one which is Greek—Philip. They are attracted by the kindred sound. Is not *this* the man to lead them to Jesus—a man with an affinity of name to the names of their own countrymen! And so Philip becomes the medium of the first Gentile wave. To him is it granted to open the door. To him is committed the privilege of unveiling the Christ to the eyes of other lands. To him, above all, is assigned the glory of performing the great marriage between the East and the West, and of joining the hand of Europe to the hand of Asia!

Was there any fruit of this union? Did the meeting of Philip with the Greeks produce any effect on history? Let me hazard a suggestion—a suggestion which, so far as I know, has not been made before, but which has long been graven on my own mind.

Some years afterwards there appeared in the Christian world a young man of great power and promise. He was a Greek of Jewish descent, and his name was also Philip. Like the elder Philip, he too was commanded to work in a desert—a place where to all appearance no bread could be found. Yet it was found — in rich superabundance. In that desert he met only one man whom he could make a Christian; but that one man was the centre of a whole kingdom—the bread was multiplied indefinitely. Now, I have always believed that this second Philip received his name at baptism in honour of the first. I have always believed that he was one of those Greeks who came to the Christian apostle with the intention of seeing the Lord. I have figured to myself the result of that vision. I have seen this youth baptised into the new faith, and in the strength of gratitude taking the name of his patron. I have seen him go forth fired with the enthusiasm of spreading that faith among his countrymen. I have seen him, after the death of Stephen, emerge as the champion of these countrymen and claim their rights in the Christian community. Then I have seen his sympathies widen — go beyond Greece, pass into Samaria, travel into Ethiopia, move wherever the spirit prompted him. If the life of such a man was the fruit of the visit to the apostle Philip, the ministry of that apostle was abundantly blessed.

LORD, often, like Philip, I have been underrating my surroundings. I have been complaining of my prosaic sphere; I have been saying, 'Whence shall I find bread in this wilderness to feed the multitude of men!' I have been looking for aid to an opening in the heavens—to the descent of powers supernal. It never occurred to me that one loaf of bread could be multiplied into a million. It never entered into my mind that one man could be an army, one life a kingdom, one soul a generation. But

Thou hast taught me, O my Father. Thou hast shown me the triumph of my trifles, the majesty of my rejected moments. The hour over which I wept is waving with banners. The book over which I slept is surging with songs. The fence over which I leapt is laden with pearls. My fancied weed has become a flower; my imagined prison has become a bower; my supposed weakness has become a tower. Evermore let me reverence the prosaic things! Evermore let me uncover my head to the place that seems a desert! Let me walk with solemnity beside the rill!—it may be a river one day. Let me tread with awe the village street!—it may be a city one day. Let me stand with veneration before the squalid child!—he may be a Shakespeare one day. Once, with proud foot I passed a hovel by; I was in search of great events, and I lingered not. And lo! I had passed the great event of Thy world—the babe whose swaddling bands were to enfold all nations! The gold and the frankincense and the myrrh were there, and the motherhood that taught

Thy fatherhood, and the wisdom that had found a new worship, and the star that had lit a new hope! When I am tempted to despise the desert, let me remember, O Lord, the majesty of the manger!

9

Matthew the Exalted

THERE is nothing more striking in the Christian Gallery than the variety in its modes of redemption. Christ produces a revolution in every soul with which He comes into contact; and yet in no two cases is the revolution precisely the same. Human weakness is as varied in its forms as human virtue; therefore the cure of human weakness must be also varied. In the figures which have already passed before us we must have been struck beyond everything with the absence of uniformity in their disease and its treatment. We have not found any two of them alike in the symptoms which needed to be healed. There is no analogy between the original defect of John the Baptist and the original defect of John the Evangelist; the one is the narrowness of personal zeal, the other the narrowness of personal pride. There is no resemblance between the imperfect views of Nathanael and the imperfect views of Nicodemus; the former come from rustic simplicity, the latter from scholarly culture. There is no parallel between the cloud in the mind of Peter and the cloud in the mind of Thomas; the one comes from want of courage, the other purely from want of hope.

I am now approaching a figure of the group whose prominent feature is just the fact of his redemption—Matthew the Publican. Our first impression is that we must expect to find this man without any *special* weakness, but encrusted with a mass of sin all over. We can put our hand upon the error which signalised the Baptist. We can point to the fault which distinguished the evangelist John. We can indicate the weakness which marred the progress of Peter. We can tell the beset-ting frailties which lent struggle to the lives of Philip and Thomas and Nicodemus. But if we were asked to specialise the fault of Matthew, I think we should say, 'You might as well ask me to specialise the fault of a quagmire!' We look on this man, not as one with a besetting sin, but as one who had sin for his very essence. I went into a country church one day and heard the character of Matthew expounded as if his badness were a truism. He was everything that was wicked—an extortioner, a cheat, a defrauder, a liar, a man dishonest in thought and word and deed. Here was a character with no specially besetting sin. You could not label him. You could label Peter or John or Thomas, but not Matthew; he was a quagmire—he was pollution all round.

Now, let me say at once that this is not the view I have taken of the matter. I think Matthew was a man with a special defect—not with pollution all over. The latter supposition is negatived partly by the fact of his call and mainly by his immediate response to that call. It was a call, not to mere mercy, but to the height of apostolic dignity. I could understand a man like Judas becoming

depraved subsequent to ordination; but I
cannot understand a man called to ordination
at a time when he was already depraved.
And if I am reminded how the heart can
conceal its vices, still less can I understand
how a heart with such vices could *care* for
such ordination—how a man of extortion, of
fraud, of covetousness, of avarice without
principle and greed without justice, could in
a moment, in the twinkling of an eye, give
up his entire world and join the ranks of
poverty. I have already said, in speaking of
the transition into a new life, that the actual
plunge is ever sudden; but I have also said
that there is a long walk to the river-side.
A conversion like this would have been to
Matthew an experience of the plunge without
the walk.

And what is the evidence on which rests the
unqualified badness of Matthew? It is the
obloquy attached to his profession. The
preacher says: 'This man was a publican—
one of those who farmed the taxes for the
Roman government. Those who farmed the

taxes were selected from the lowest social strata. They were originally poor, hungry, ill-clad. The occupation, therefore, to which they were chosen placed them in a sphere of strong temptation. They had every induce-ment to be unjust, to overreach, to exact, to falsify, to become the instruments for bribery and corruption. And Matthew was one of these. He was a member of this fraternity, immersed in a trade which held out a prospect of gain to the unscrupulous and offered a life of comfort to him who did not resist the tempter. Surely a record like his could have only one issue!'

The logic of this is deplorable. It is equiva-lent to saying that, if a man belongs to a calling which involves a particular tempta-tion, he must be held guilty of having yielded to that temptation. Consider for a moment. There is no profession known to me which does not involve its own special temptation. The clerical calling tempts to narrowness, the medical to materialism, the legal to the loss of sentiment, the literary to a spirit of selfishness.

Yet one of the broadest men **I** ever knew was a sincerely orthodox cleric; one of the most assured Christians I ever knew was a leading physician; one of the most kindly sympathisers I ever knew was a legal practitioner; one of the most sacrificing lives I ever knew was a highly successful writer. We must protest against attributing to any man the special sin of his calling. It is unfair; it is negatived by a thousand facts. There was nothing in Roman tax-gathering which made vice in that calling a necessary thing. In point of fact, the vice came from the outside. The *master*-publicans were men of rank and credit; but they put their work into the hands of subordinates who were often taken from the slums. The vices these exhibited in their profession were brought with them *into* their profession; they came from the previous corruptions of human nature, and no trade is chargeable with them. We cannot morally label Matthew by calling him 'Matthew the Publican.'

The truth is, the obloquy with which

Matthew was regarded by his countrymen did not proceed from the fear that he was a bad man, but from the certainty that he was a bad Jew. The most galling fact to the Israel of later days was the fact that she paid tribute to another land. Ideally, she claimed to be the mistress of the world—the nation into whose treasury all tribute should flow. To the proud eye of the prophet Isaiah, she had been the mountain established on the top of the hills, and toward her height the other lands had looked, wondering. That such a nation should pay taxes to a foreign people, a Gentile people, was an awful thought. It was a pain worse than laceration, more cruel than a blow. But there was the possibility of a pain more poignant still. It was bad enough that the tribute of homage from Israel should be collected by a *Roman*. But what if the man who gathered it should be a son of Israel herself—a scion of her race, an heir to her promises, a nursling of her prophets! What if the man who taunted her with her misfortunes should be one born within her pale, bred within her precincts, sheltered within her privileges—one from whom was due the veneration for her sanctuary and the reverence for her God! Would it not seem to her as if all her calamities had culminated and as if the cloud of her sorrow had deepened into starless night!

Now, this often happened; and it happened in the case of Matthew. Here was a Jew who had lost the last shred of patriotism! He had forgotten the traditions of his ancestors—forgotten the parted waters of the Red Sea, and the burning bush, and the pillars of cloud and fire! He had become oblivious that he was the son of a race which claimed the ultimate dominion over all the world! He had not only accepted without a blush the domination by the stranger; he had taken part with the stranger in his domination! He had attached himself to the enemies of his country—had become a collector of their tribute from his own conquered land! This was hard upon that land. The man who acted thus was bound to be execrated by his race. He was execrated on that ground alone. No amount of personal vices would in the eyes of his countrymen have added to the enormity of his sin, and no amount of personal virtues would in the slightest degree have minimised that sin.   His deed was itself to them the acme of all iniquity, from which nothing could detract and which nothing could intensify. The blackness of Matthew's character in the eyes of the Jew was the fact of his apostasy.

But the question is, What is its blackness in *our* eyes?   We sympathise much with the feeling of his countrymen; yet, after all, that is a local matter, and the question should be viewed apart from local considerations. We must ask ourselves, Where lay the precise fault in this absence of patriotism? When we have answered that, we shall have found the real weak point in the character of Matthew — the point which made him an object for Christ's compassion, and the point which suggested Christ's mode of cure.

It is quite evident to me that a defect in Jewish patriotism always proceeded from one definite defect in character—a want of self-respect. I do not say that every man who has lost his patriotism has lost his self-respect, for every man's country is not meant to be identical with his own soul. But the Jew's was. I have already said in speaking of Nicodemus that in the Jewish community the nation and the individual were one. A man's loves and fears were for his native land. His land was a part of himself—the largest part; its preservation was his main motive for living. A Jew could only forget his country by ceasing to care for himself—by losing self-respect. All in him that was personal was national—his feasts, his sacrifices, his family, his hopes, his sins, his sorrows, his very aspirings after immortality. To destroy within his heart the care for his country was to destroy within his heart all care for anything.

Here, then, is the real source of Matthew's want of patriotism; it is want of self-respect. His defect is the extreme opposite of that which we found in the original nature of the evangelist John. John, as I have indicated, had too big a mirror; Matthew had no mirror at all. John saw his youthful figure at an exaggerated height; Matthew beheld no reflection of himself whatever. John required to have his glass smashed; Matthew needed to have a glass constructed. John had too much pride; Matthew had too little. It would be difficult to say which of the extremes is the more fraught with danger —the excess of self-respect or the absence of self-respect. Too steadfast a gaze at self has slain its thousands; but it may be doubted if the *failure* to see one's self has not produced as many victims. Pride is a positive state; want of self-respect is a negative state. But I think the mind suffers as much by its moments of negation as by its moments of positive evil. The heart filled with personal vanity is not safe; but the heart unfilled by any personal interest is no safer. There are in my opinion as many young men led astray by the want of a looking-glass as by the over-prominence of a looking-glass. It is a dangerous thing when we express a real truth by the words, ' I do not care.'

I have said that the want of self-respect
is in itself a negative quality. I wish to
emphasise the point, because it is often mistaken for things from which it is quite different.
For instance, we associate this quality with
meanness. Yet the mean man is never without his mirror. He errs, not by want of
self-respect, but by a low ideal of what in
the self is respectable. He sees himself in
the glass adorned in purple and fine linen
and faring sumptuously every day. He says,
'*This* is "to live," *this* is "to prosper," *this*
is "to be respected"!' Then follows the
conclusion, 'This is the only thing worth
striving for; let me work for nothing else,
aim at nothing else, dream of nothing else;
let me seek wealth at all times and by all
means!'

Will any man say that such a soul is in
want of a mirror! Does its meanness not
come from its mirror—from the sight of a
false ideal of what it is to be great! Such a
soul has reached its dishonesties, its frauds,
its extortions, its unjust dealings, by nothing

else than a mode of self-contemplation—by gazing into a glass which paints the little as if it were the grand. If Matthew had lost his Jewish patriotism, he was *not* that man, for he who lost his Jewish patriotism lost his glass too, and had no longer an aim in life either high or low.

Again. We often associate want of self-respect with abjectness. By abjectness I mean one's feeling that he is a poor creature —that he is a worm and no man. And yet this condition is also incompatible with the loss of the mirror. It is itself a looking into the glass. It is by the reflection in that glass I come to the conclusion that I *am* a poor creature. The word 'self-respect' literally means self-regarding, self-beholding. In the case of the crushed or abject man, he beholds himself as an object of compassion, as a thing worthy to win pity, as one who deserved a better fate. The man who has lost his mirror cannot be an abject man. That would be a contradiction in terms; he would have no shadow of himself to look at, and so could not grieve over it. Matthew was not an abject man. Not even after his call does he sit in sackcloth and ashes over the memory of his past. On the contrary, he makes a great feast in his own house and invites his fellow-publicans. The act could never have proceeded from one beholding his natural face in a glass.

What, then, is the bane of having no mirror? It is being down without knowing it. It is the living by the day—without a plan, without a principle. It is a vegetable life. It is the absence of all desire to look forward to anything, to look backward to anything, to look upward to anything. It is the enclosure within the moment. It is the experience of a state of mind which may not always be doing harm, but which is never doing good. It may keep the precepts, 'Thou shalt not kill,' 'Thou shalt not steal,' 'Thou shalt not bear false witness'; but it will have no impulse to seek and to save, no bosom on which to lay the burdens of humanity.

What, therefore, did Matthew need? It was

a mirror—a sense of exaltation. It is not enough that a man has no depression; he must have exaltation. I will go further. I think that in spiritual matters the valley is nearer to the mountain than is the plain. I believe that a life of conscious depression will sooner reach the sense of a height than a life of commonplace prosaic routine which looks neither up nor down. Matthew was a man of the plain. He was not, like Thomas, a man of the valley. Thomas had depression, in other words, he saw himself in a glass and pitied himself. But Matthew had no depression. His was not a valley experience. He lived on level ground without depths or heights. He never saw *himself*—he had no mirror. To have a mirror you must be either on the mountain or in the vale; Matthew's was as yet a plant's life. Jesus said, ' I must give this man a sight of his higher self, of his possible self.' He felt that what Matthew needed was a stimulus—something to lift him up. There were those to whom He came with a cross—those who, like the woman of

Samaria, had to be wakened to their own shame. But to this man He came with a crown. What Matthew needed to feel was his own importance. Let him be lifted up to the mountain—suddenly, drastically, unexpectedly. Let him get a sight of his future self, what he is coming to, what is coming to him. Let him see himself as God meant him to be—a man of dignity, a man of power. That was what Jesus did to Matthew the Publican. He came without warning, without preparation. He stood before him at the receipt of custom. He ignored all the crowd assembled there. He fixed His gaze upon him alone—apart from his fellows, apart from the yielders of his tribute. He addressed him without preamble, without title—as if He were summing up a long process of reasoning; He said, bluntly and boldly, 'Follow Me!'

For the first time in his life Matthew found himself a *man*—a man of importance, a man of mark. He awoke to find himself famous —an object of interest, a centre of attraction.

He had the novel experience of standing with a mirror in his hand looking at his own person. So novel was the experience that it carried him away. Surprise overmastered him. That Christ should choose *him* — the cipher, the nobody, the man who had forfeited his right to call himself a son of Israel — this was a startling thing. That he, who had never been dignified enough to care what the world might think of him, should be suddenly called to stand before the world as an example, was a thought almost weird in its strangeness. The newness of the sensation quite conquered him. 'Follow Me!' said the voice; and he lingered not a moment. He did not wait for enlightenment; he had got the one light whose absence had made him ignoble—self-respect. His exodus came with his exaltation. The instant he said, 'I am somebody,' he rose and left Egypt. He went out from the receipt of custom and passed over into the Christian land. Like Israel, he made his 'passover' a subject of congratulation. Our last glimpse of him but one is at that banquet which he spread as a farewell to the old and an in-auguration of the new.

But there is one glimpse more, and it is to me the most suggestive of all. The next time we see Matthew he has a pen in his hand; he is writing a gospel. Volumes have been multiplied on that gospel. Discussions have been reiterated as to the source of its materials and the origin of its information. Commentaries have been accumulated ex-hausting every possible meaning of his words and embodying every thought involved in his teaching. It would seem as if the subject were at last threadbare. And yet there is one fact about this gospel which, so far as I know, has never been spoken—its connection with Matthew's call. We are in the habit of regarding it as a purely impersonal piece of writing—without any note of autobiography or incidental emergence of the author's memory. The truth, as I believe, is that the very central idea of the book is itself a note of autobio-graphy. What is that central idea? It is the spirit of patriotism. The Gospel of Matthew is the most patriotic of all the gospels. His Christ is the Christ of Israel—born king of the Jews. All that He does is made to echo the glories of Matthew's native land. Everything about Him is the flowering of Israel's prophecies, is done 'that it might be fulfilled which was spoken.' The glory of Messiah is that He has glorified this favoured nation— proved that she was right in her aspirations and in her dreams. This patriotism of the First Gospel is of course known to every schoolboy. But have we considered what it means in relation to the character of Matthew himself? Nothing less than a moral revolution. This man's defect had all along been a want of patriotism. He had ignored the claims of his country, he had disregarded the ties of his people. But, when for the last time our eyes rest upon him, he is a man transformed. He has become rich just where he was poor, overflowing just where he was deficient. He is a patriot of the patriots. His country which yesterday was nothing is to-day all in all. He has put on the arms of his race—is prepared to fight for it, to die for it. He has declared himself a son of Israel and is ready to lavish on her all his praise.

And I think there is something very grand and very beautiful in this final glimpse which we receive of Matthew the Publican. It is our glimpse of one who has got back his self-respect and longs to atone. He has been for years denuding his country of her due. He now says, 'I must make it up to her at last, though late; I must compensate her for the gifts I have withheld!' I say there is something fine in this man's light at evening-time. Though it *is* evening, though the day is far spent, though many golden hours and golden opportunities have been lost, he will not despair of undoing his past. He will concentrate into the evening sky what he should have spread over the whole day. He will bestow his gifts in double measure. He will assign to his native land a glory which he could not, even if he would, have given in his morning hours. For now the Christ has come—Judah has received her latest flower. He can tell her of that flower, can tell her of her share in its production. He can tell her how she has been justified, glorified, raised out of the category of vain dreamers and proclaimed to be a nation which has a star in heaven. That is why Matthew in the evening writes his life of Jesus.

LORD, teach me the dignity of my own soul! Many have warned me of the pride of life; and it is evil and harmful indeed. But I think an equal danger has come from my hours of recklessness. I think I have never been further from Thee than in the moment when I have said, 'Life is a worthless thing!' Whenever I go out without my mirror I am very near temptation. When I say in my heart, 'It will be all the same a hundred years hence,' I am perilously close to the precipice. In that moment I have broken my mirror—have lost sight of life's magnitude, life's value. When I lose the sight of life's value, I begin to value lower things; when I break my mirror, I look into the muddy pool. My Father, I think it is for idle *hearts* that

Satan finds mischief. Save me from an idle heart—a heart that has nothing to love! If my heart has its mirror, yea, even its mirror of care, I shall not touch the miry clay. All idleness is the heart's idleness—the heart ceasing to vibrate. Though my hands be folded, though my lips be silent, though my feet be resting, though my fancy be reposing, yet, if my heart be carrying its mirror, I am not idle. Keep that glass undimmed, O my Father! Whatever else I lose, let me never lose my love —the sense that life holds something dear! Let no cloud curtain it! Let no storm sink it! Let no waters wash it away! May every beam brighten it! May every hope hallow it! May every fear freshen it! May every dream deepen it! May every cross crown it! May every rock rivet it! May every struggle strengthen it! May every providence purify it! May it be my star in night, my song in stillness, my flower in winter, my rainbow in tears, my help in sorrow, my home in exile, my youth in autumn, my island in the sea! **Never let my heart drop the mirror of its glory!**

10

Zaccheus the Conscience-struck

THE name of Zaccheus occupies only a few
verses of St. Luke's Gospel. It does not occur
in any other Gospel, and throughout the Scriptures it is never mentioned again. But a
man's place in the Gallery is by no means
determined by his prominence in the Record.
What decides a man's place in the Gallery is
his uniqueness. Is there anything in his face
or figure which separates him from all the
surrounding portraits? If there is, then, however seldom he may be alluded to, he is
entitled to a prominent position in the Scripture Gallery; if there is not, then, however
frequent be the recurrence of his name, he has
no right to a distinctive place. The question
is, Has Zaccheus anything new to say—anything that has not been said by Peter or John

or Philip or Thomas or Nathanael? Is the phase of Christianity which he expresses different from the phases which have been previously expressed? Does he stand for a class which has not been already accounted for; does he represent a section of mankind who have as yet received no spokesman? Then is he amply entitled to occupy a front ground in that great collection of portraits which has conveyed to all times the separate phases of the Christian life.

And I say that Zaccheus is such a man. He flashes out a new shade of colour in the Great Gallery. He is not exactly like any of his predecessors. The nearest approach to him is Matthew—both were publicans. Yet, unlike Matthew, Zaccheus was not an object of personal recrimination to his countrymen. He was not, as Matthew was, a subordinate who collected the taxes. He was a *master*-publican —a rich man living in Jericho who simply estimated the revenues and reported them to the government. The fruits of his conversion no doubt resembled those brought forth by

Matthew, and this is easily explained by the identity of their professions. But the men originally were very different. Matthew was a man with no interest in life; Zaccheus is essentially the reverse—a man of curiosity. Matthew had slow pulses; the heart of Zaccheus beat rapidly. Matthew needed to be *called*; Zaccheus took the initiative. Matthew required stirring up; Zaccheus would run a race or climb a tree in the eagerness to secure his object.

If I were asked to state in a sentence what Zaccheus represents, I should say he stands for the average man wakened by conscience. Hitherto in this Gallery we have not seen the average man. We have seen men whose likeness will be found in every age and clime; but *that* does not make one an average man. Peculiarities may be *reproduced* in every age and clime; but they will not be reproduced over the whole mass. Peter is not an average man; he is the specimen of a type of mind. John is not an average man; he is the representative of a class. Nathanael and Nicodemus and Thomas and Philip are not average men; they stand for particular phases of human nature. But Zaccheus belongs to the majority. There is nothing peculiar about him, nothing marked, nothing uncommon. His special feature is his want of specialty; it is a feature which we have never met before, and which in the remaining figures we shall not meet again. Everything about his character is middle-sized. Physically, he is of short stature; but mentally, he is neither short nor tall. He is neither a paragon of excellence nor a monster of wickedness. He is not a hero and he is not a demon. He has many good points, but they never blaze; he has many bad points, but they never freeze. He is the average man. He is as virtuous as his neighbours. He never transgresses use and wont. He does nothing wrong in the way of business for which he cannot quote a precedent. He may overleap the laws of rectitude; but he would be miserable to be told that he had violated the mercantile standard of those around him. He lives up to his own measurement; but he measures himself by the mass.

Such is my reading of the original character of Zaccheus. He was a man who was always standing before a judgment-throne to give an account of what he had done; but it was not the judgment-throne of Christ. It was the throne of public opinion before which he stood—the standard of those within his immediate environment. When he transgressed that tribunal, his conscience troubled him; but the tribunal itself was a very inferior one—his conscience ought to have demanded more. What he needed was to have his conscience placed at the bar of a higher throne of judgment. He required to see a loftier ideal, to feel the presence of a more exacting law. Our first impression is that a man of such a comparatively correct life is favourable soil for the planting of Christian seed. It appears easier to convert him than one who is down in the depths. But I think this impression is erroneous. There is none so difficult to move upward as the average man—none whom it is so hard to quicken into a Christian conscience. And the reason is that the man has a conscience already of a very keen though very inferior stamp. The tribunal of public opinion blunts him to every other tribunal. He is lulled into complacency. The judgment-throne is low-set, but it is the highest he has known, and it has been his standard through life. He has always reverenced the average—the golden mean. Christianity makes its appeal to something abnormal—to those who feel as if they were *below* the average, as if they were the chief of sinners, as if they could only beat upon their breast and cry, 'Unclean!' The man who lives in Jericho and is content with the consciousness that he is up to the average life of Jericho has a natural disqualification for meeting Christ—the disqualification of those who think they have already attained.

What enabled Zaccheus to surmount this natural barrier? Strange to say, it was the fact that his religious deficiency was counterbalanced by a purely secular impulse—the spirit of curiosity. The picture as delineated in the Gallery is graphic. Jesus is coming to Jericho, and Jericho is on fire with expectation. His fame has gone before Him. Crowds have gathered in the streets to await His arrival—anxious inquirers about the health of body or soul. Zaccheus is anxious neither about body nor soul ; but he is eager to *see.* If he has any concern, it is about his physical limitations. How shall a small man like him be able to procure a sight of Jesus with such a dense phalanx in front of him ! An idea strikes him. He feels sure that Jesus will not address the people while they are in the streets —He will advance into the open and let the multitude follow Him. Little Zaccheus will get ahead of them. He will run before into the woodlands and climb up to the branch of a tree, where his small stature will be compensated by artificial height and he will see over the heads of taller men.

Now, I venture to say that in all the Gospel narrative this is a unique approach to the person of Christ. All the others were either answers to His own invitation or advances of the sufferer impelled by human pain. Here is a man who has not been called and who has not been afflicted. He has neither been summoned from the receipt of custom like Matthew nor driven by the burden of sorrow like Jairus. He has no ailment about him, no depression about him. He is alive with the spirit of youth, and he is brought by an impulse which is the very index of the youthful spirit—curiosity. Unique as it is in the Gospel, it is ever the approach of the average man towards every great and good thing. It is the child's attraction to school, the boy's attraction to knowledge, the youth's attraction to travel, the man's attraction to nature. Announce a descriptive lecture on Palestine illustrated by the magic-lantern, and the young people will come in crowds. They will not be drawn by the promised description nor even by the promised illustration of it—an interest in Palestine requires mental development. They will be attracted by the magic-lantern itself; the scenes depicted will be interesting not as scenes of Palestine, but as feats of pictorial transformation. Yet, who does not see that in the future the memory of these things will become grapes of Eshcol. What is now a mere source of curiosity will come to the mature mind as a hallowed re- membrance clothing in form and colour those spots of sacred story which would otherwise convey nothing but a name.

Zaccheus came to the temple of Christian truth as the average man is led to all truth— on the wings of curiosity. His was apparently the lowest motive in all that crowd. Yet he is singled out as if he were the hero of the crowd. To him, sitting in his sycamore tree, the voice of Jesus cries, ' Make haste, Zaccheus, and come down, for to-day I must abide at thy house.' The favour is so great, and the privilege so well-nigh unparalleled, that we are tempted to ask if we have not underrated the spirit of curiosity. Surely the Master must have seen in this man's motive some- thing more than we see—something which placed him on a higher level than those who had come to be cured of bodily maladies!

Can it be that there is after all a mental element in curiosity—an element which is indicative of the character and predictive of the life! Let us see.

There is to my mind a great resemblance between the spirit of curiosity and the spirit of prayer. Neither of them is in itself either good or bad; it depends on what you are curious about, it depends on what you are in want of. Prayer may be of three kinds—immoral, non-moral, or moral. If I ask for vengeance on an enemy, that is immoral prayer. If I ask for a chariot and horses, that is non-moral prayer—it is neither saintly nor sinful, but purely secular. If I ask to be made holy, harmless, and undefiled, that is moral prayer—it is a sign of incipient purity. So, also, there are three kinds of curiosity—immoral, non-moral, and moral. If I am eager to see a bull-fight, that is immoral curiosity—it is a wish to view pain. If I am eager to see a man who professes to lift heavy weights, that is non-moral curiosity — it is neither good nor bad. If I am eager to hear a great preacher who has for months been attracting crowds around him, then, even though it may be accompanied by no anxiety about my spiritual state, that is moral curiosity —it indicates a listening attitude in the human soul and the presence of an open door.

I do not wonder, then, that Zaccheus was singled out from the multitude. His body was on a sycamore tree and was therefore easily distinguishable. But his soul was also on a sycamore tree—raised above the crowd. His very physical elevation, separating him as it did from outward contact with Jesus, showed that he wanted nothing physical—that his motive was curiosity of mind. I do not wonder that this approach, prayerless as it was, impersonal as it was, unsolicitous as it was, made an impression on Jesus beyond the common cries for bread and sustenance. It was like the impression made on Him by Thomas. But Thomas came with low hope —if he asked nothing it was because he expected nothing. Zaccheus had the spirit of youth; his hopes were high; only, they were mental hopes. He swung up his little body beyond the reach of temporal help; but he bent the eye of his soul upon the vision of Jesus. What he wanted to see was a spiritual glory, and Christ rated the man according to his desire. He picked him out from the mass and said, ' I must abide at thy house to-day.'

I wish here to direct attention to a frequent peculiarity in the method of Jesus. When He is about to confer a favour on any one, He often begins by asking a favour from *him*. However dimly Zaccheus is aware of his mental need, Jesus knows it very well and is prepared to remedy it. Yet, instead of telling him that he is a poor creature requiring Divine aid, He asks aid *from* him. He says, ' I require shelter to-night; no house will be so convenient for me as yours; can you give me room?' We see the same thing in the case of the woman of Samaria, where He begins by asking a drink of water. We see it in the case of Magdalene, where He allows her service to precede His cure. We see it in His acceptance of the invitation to abide at

Emmaus. We see it in His receiving of hospitality at many a feast. We see it in His submission to the outpouring on His person of the costliest ointment, and in His willingness to partake of material comforts from the hands of the women of Galilee.

These facts are not accidental. They are a part of the deep moral insight of Jesus. What is the relation which He wishes to establish between Himself and His followers? It is one of communion. Now, communion cannot be on one side. It is not possible that such a relation can exist between any two minds if the one is active and the other passive. There is nothing so paralysing as the perpetual receiving of benefits. Even in a case of forgiveness the delinquent should be allowed to do something for his pardoner. If I have offended you, there is a breach between us; and that breach is not healed by the mere fact that you forgive me. Even after the forgiveness, I am still in the valley and you on the mount. It is not enough that you descend to me; I must be allowed to meet you half-way. Pardon is not reconciliation. In one sense it is the reverse of reconciliation, for it emphasises the difference between your height and my depth. Reconciliation seeks to abolish that difference. It aims to break inequality, to restore communion. It cannot restore communion while the sacrifice is all on one side. I who am pardoned must be suffered to do something for you the pardoner. It is not enough that you bring forth the best robe and put it on me; I must be allowed to give a garment to *you*. Christ is coming to pardon Zaccheus; but He does not want this pardon to leave Zaccheus in the valley. He desires him to have a memory that he too was the bestower of a gift, that he was able to extend a courtesy in return for favours received. And so, with a fine touch of gracefulness, He makes it appear as if the favour were to *Him*. He asks hospitality, shelter, companionship for the day. As He had begged the Samaritan for a draught from the well, He begs Zaccheus to make Him a guest for the hour; and in both cases for the same reason—that the mind, before its vision, may have a sense of independent dignity.

Jesus, then, became for one day the guest of Zaccheus; and at the evening-time there dawned for him a great light. It was a light which rose upon his conscience. He stood before a new judgment-seat; and there sat on it 'one like unto a son of man.' Hitherto, the arbiter of his conscience had been public opinion. Suddenly public opinion became valueless. All the social magnets fled from his throne, and in their place there stood one solitary figure wielding the sceptre over his heart and giving the law to his life. In the morning he had said, 'How will society regard me?' in the evening his question is, 'What will Jesus say?' In the morning he was comforted by the low standard of a multitude; in the evening he is ruffled by the lofty standard of One. In the morning he was self-complacent by viewing the numbers on his own road; in the evening he is perturbed by the sight of a single individual on the summit of a commanding hill.

Yet, there is something startling about this revival in the conscience of Zaccheus. It is not exactly what we should expect. We expect to see an awakened man bow his head and cry, 'Lord, be merciful to me, a sinner !' Zaccheus feels himself to be in moral debt ; but, strange to say, it is to man. He has two cries of remorse ; but they are both for the human. He feels he has done too little good, and he feels he has done too much bad. He wants to remedy both—the one by charity and the other by compensation, 'The half of my goods I give to the poor, and if I have taken any thing from any man by false accusation, I restore him fourfold.' We hear the same double cry from the lips of Matthew ; he makes a feast to express his charity, and he writes a Gospel to redeem his want of patriotism. But the strange thing is that these men should not have first wished to put themselves right with *God*. When David kills Uriah, he takes a theological view of the matter, and cries, in the psalm traditionally attributed to him, 'Against Thee, Thee only, have I sinned, and

done this evil in *Thy* sight.' Why should
Zaccheus take a *human* view of the matter!
Why should he allow the injury to his fellow-
creatures to obscure his sense of an offended
Lawgiver! Why should he look with dismay
on what he has failed to do and what he has
done amiss for humanity when there is another
and a graver subject which should press upon
his thoughts—his violation of the statutes of
heaven, his breaking of the commandments of
God!

But look deeper. Do you suppose Zaccheus
thought this 'another subject'! Do you think
that when he lamented his shortcomings towards his fellow-men he regarded himself in
any other light than as a transgressor of
Divine law! Remember into what he had
been baptised that day! He had accepted a
new definition of God—had said, 'God is love.'
What did that mean? It meant that for him
in all time to come the law of God was broken
when the rights of man were violated. It
meant that to outrage the justice of God was
to trample on the heart of his brothers. It

meant that to leave poverty unassisted, to pass privation unpitied, to turn aside from the sight of struggle and pain, was to commit sacrilege against the Divine mercy-seat, to stain the steps of the altar of sacrifice. It meant that, if Zaccheus were conscious of an unpaid debt to man, it was really the consciousness of an unpaid debt to God, and that the road to atonement with God was through the rehabilitation of man. That was the new view which burst upon the soul of this man of Jericho. It was a view which embodied the whole doctrine of the coming Calvary. It taught that the way to reconciliation with the Father is to lay down life for the brethren, and that to atone for past sin is to bear the cross of humanity. It was really an annulling of the distinction between the secular and the sacred. To the eye of Zaccheus all duties became church duties. His receipt of custom became a Divine service to be piously performed. The exchange took the sanctity of a temple. The gifts bestowed upon the widow and the orphan were treasures lent to the

Lord. The coin laid on the lap of poverty was a holy offering to heaven. The raising of a life from secular want and temporal despair was the building of a new synagogue which one day might be fit for the habitation of the King of kings.

And this union of the secular and the sacred within the heart of Zaccheus explains something which separates his call from most other Gospel calls—which gives it an aspect more consonant with modern than with ancient life. When Christ summoned men to join His standard, the obedience to the summons commonly involved a change of occupation. 'We have left all, and followed Thee' is the cry of the disciples. The fishermen of Galilee were transformed into fishers of human souls ; Peter, Andrew, James, John, Philip, forsook their nets when they became members of the league of pity. Matthew himself, whose case is the most analogous to that of Zaccheus, is called out of his profession ; he leaves the business of tax-gathering when he follows Jesus. But Zaccheus gets no such command. The change

wrought in him is all within. He is not told
to give up his trade, to abandon his daily
resorts, to quit the exchange and the market-
place. He is not led to think that the em-
ployment he has been pursuing is common
or unclean. Rather does there flash upon him
the knowledge that he has been polluting that
which is holy, staining that which is sacred,
soiling that which is Divine. There breaks
upon him the conviction that to be a good
man he needs not the wings of a dove to fly
away—that he may stand *here* and be holy,
work *here* and be pure, toil amid the perishable
things of time and yet perform the deeds of
a saint of the Most High. I think there is
something very fine in the fact that, amid the
many Gospel pictures of men leaving the old
world to win the new, there is one which
depicts a human soul in a different attitude—
as impregnating with its own purity the things
among which all along it has lived and moved
and had its being.

ABIDE in my house one day, O Son of
Man! A voice has sung in Thy praise,
'I triumph still if Thou abide with me.' Yet
it is not for the triumph I need Thine abiding;
it is rather for the overshadowing of my too-
triumphant self. I am ever triumphant in
myself when Thou art *not* with me. I am like
the artist that has never seen a picture but
his own. He is very proud of his own, for
he has no artistic conscience to see its
blemishes. He will never be great till he sees
its blemishes—till one of the master-painters
come and 'abide' with him. I too am without
conscience till Thy coming. I cannot see my
spots till the sun rise. It is not my blemishes
which drive me to Thy light; it is Thy light
which drives me to my blemishes. Never can
I learn the poverty of my own painting until
Thy portrait is hung upon my wall. Then my
true conscience will be born; then shall I
realise my own nothingness. From Thy light
shall come my loathing; from Thy beauty
shall come my burden; from Thy song shall
come my sigh. I shall be dissatisfied in the

dawn. I shall be humbled on the height. I shall be convicted when I put on the crown. Rise upon my night that I may *know* my night! Sing in my silence that I may search my silence! Shine in my heart that I may hate my heart! Flood me with Thy love that I may learn my lovelessness! Touch me with Thy peace that I may perceive my pain! Take me up to the mount, O Lord, take me up to the mount! for only in Thy pure air shall I find my foulness, and only in an upper room shall I discover the depth below. I shall cease to triumph in myself if Thou shalt 'abide with me.'

11

James the Softened

ALL the figures we have been considering have been men of the spring. What I mean is that they recognised a power in Christ the moment He was presented to them. They may have erred as to where that power lay— Nicodemus may have seen it too much in the physical, Thomas too little; but a power of some kind they all *at once* recognised. We are coming now, however, to a figure which reveals an exception to the rule; it is that of James the Lord's brother. I would call him distinctively the man of the autumn. It is not that in point of time he was late in becoming a Christian—in years he was young when he joined the cause of Christ. But he was old in experience. He had resisted the Christian influence longer than any of his apostolic contemporaries. And the fact is more remarkable because outwardly he was more privileged than any of these. He was a member of Christ's own family—probably an inmate of His home at Nazareth. He is called 'the Lord's brother.' What that means I shall not here discuss. Whether he was a cousin of Jesus, whether he was the child of Joseph by a former marriage, or whether he was a son of Mary subsequent to the birth at Bethlehem, has been keenly disputed. Personally, I lean to the last view. But the point here is that, whichever view we take, this man had outward opportunities of contact with Jesus such as were not enjoyed by any of his comrades. In spite of that, he seems at first to have been as great an unbeliever as Saul of Tarsus. There has always been to me a deep significance in that saying of St. John that the followers of Christ were 'not born of blood.' He must have had in his mind the fact that physical consanguinity had been proved in the case of Jesus to be no advantage to a man—that one could have family affinity with Him, live in the same house with Him, sit at the same board with Him, engage in the same work with Him, listen to His conversation on the most familiar topics of every day, and yet be further away from Him than a Matthew at the receipt of custom or a Nicodemus in the midst of the Sanhedrin.

You will remember also that this slowness to accept Christianity was not the result of religious indifference. It would not be too much to say that it was the result of religious intensity. There never was a young man more naturally devout than James the Lord's brother. His misfortune was that devoutness was to him identical with severity. It was essential to him that religion should be a hard thing, a painful and laborious thing. That a man should be raised into the Divine life instantaneously was for him a contradiction in terms. That the soul by a single act of faith should soar into the presence of God was in his view impossible. He was opposed to revival movements because they were rapid movements; he thought Jesus was 'beside

Himself.'[1] His idea of piety was to spend whole hours in the wrestling of prayer; tradition says that his knees had become hard by the process. God was to him a Goal whose glory consisted in not being easily won—this was the belief of his countrymen, the faith of his fathers. James had by nature a mind sternly conservative. Paul describes himself as one who had learned to be content with any circumstances he was placed in. James went further; he had learned to idolise the circumstances he was placed in. He had hardened himself against change. Even in transformed years he delighted to think of God as without 'variableness or the least shadow of turning'; originally, he delighted to think of *himself* so. He would have no innovation, no new notions, no revolutions in opinion; religion was for him something whose form was fixed once for all.

So far as I know, this state of mind continued

---

[1] So I gather from the comparison of the twenty-first and thirty-second verses of the third chapter of Mark. I regard the ' brethren ' of the later verse as identical with the ' friends ' of the former.

with James all through the earthly ministry
of Jesus. His obduracy resisted the *closest*
personal contact with the Master—a contact
extending to the minutiæ of the daily life.
But when the visible Christ was withdrawn,
when the shadows of Calvary had fallen and
the personal contact had become a thing of
the past, it was then that the revelation came.
Paul records that revelation in a brief sentence ;
he says of the departed Christ, ' He was seen
of James.' I think this vision of the departed
Christ was James's first clear seeing. To my
mind there is a strong analogy between his
experience and the experience of Paul. They
belonged to opposite schools; yet I think
there is a greater resemblance between Paul
and James than between Paul and Luke,
Paul and Silas, or Paul and Timothy. Both
were reared in rigidness. Both were opposed
to Christianity. Both were men of the autumn
—bringing in their sheaves when the day had
begun to decline. Both recognised Christ's
glory only after He had passed away from
earth. Both, after their vision, began a new

régime and became the leaders of their respective parties. There are no two men whose lives present so many points of parallel.

But the one point of difference is in the original *privilege* of James. Paul was not brought up in the companionship of Jesus; in no personal sense had he ever known Christ after the flesh. But James had; his intercourse had been of the closest. And in relation to his autumn experience, this is the difficulty to be accounted for. Paul recognised Christ whenever he saw Him; James saw Him daily without recognising Him. In this latter case the question is, Why? Why was it expedient for this man that Christ should go away, why had the night to come ere he could see Him? The man of Tarsus had no meeting on the shores of Galilee; James dwelt within the very walls which sheltered the youth of Jesus. Why is it that James was no nearer than Paul to the earthly recognition of the Son of Man?

I think you will find that there are two reasons—deeply rooted in human nature and applicable to all times. The first would sound like a paradox if it were not verified by experience. We all accept it as a truism that the great distance of one being from another is unfavourable to the *revelation* of one being to another. But it is less frequently considered that an extreme opposite case is equally unfavourable. It is less frequently considered that a very close proximity of two beings, provided the proximity has never been interrupted, is just as prejudicial to personal knowledge as would be their existence in separate lands. We are apt to think that James had a special privilege and that Paul had not. The truth is that neither had a privilege. Each had a barrier interposed between him and his Lord; but they were opposite barriers—Paul was too far away, James was too near.

That extreme nearness retards perception is a matter of daily observation. It is just as true of our perception of things as of our perception of persons. One would suppose, for example, that the habitual dwellers in a scene of rare beauty would be peculiarly alive to the attractions of physical nature. The reverse is the case. These are of all people the least responsive to the beautiful. If a stranger comes in among them, he is transfixed, dazzled, by the splendour of the scene; but his enthusiasm rather surprises them. We should suppose, again, that the constant inhabitants of a city would know more about that city than those coming into it from other places. Yet it often happens that a traveller learns more of a town in a week than many of its population learn all through their lives. We should suppose, once more, that those living continuously in a salubrious atmosphere would be free from all illness arising from atmospheric causes. Yet this is not the case. The unvaried presence of one climate is like the unvaried application of a somnolent drug —it loses its effect. A change of air will eventually be found beneficial, even though the new air be less balmy than the old. The mind must co-operate with the body to preserve the health of man. It is not enough

that an atmosphere is genial; I must feel it
to be genial. It must enter into me not only
as a draught but as a joy. And if this joy
is to be felt, it must not be an unvaried
possession. It must be interrupted to be
known; it must be withdrawn to be appre-
ciated; it must be supplanted by a shadow to
be valued as a light.

Ascend from things to persons, and you will
find a manifestation of the same principle.
It is not the inmates of one house who are
the best judges of the personality of each
other. Even such an external matter as
physical growth is most easily detected, not
by a habitual inhabitant of the same dwelling, but by one who has returned after many
days. In order to examine my brother-man
it is essential that either he or I should stand
back. The nearness disqualifies for observation. I knew a lady who had under her
charge one who was afflicted with a brain
affection. She was eager from time to time
that some test should be applied as to whether
the sufferer were mentally improving or de-

clining. But she was quite unable to apply the test herself; the fact of living constantly together made it impossible to distinguish between minute shades of mental gradation. What did she do under the circumstances? She brought the sufferer periodically to one who knew both of them, but who was living in a totally different atmosphere. His comparative distance placed him at an advantage; it enabled him to observe those indications of mental change which were altogether indiscernible by a nearer spectator.

We arrive, then, at the conclusion that, for acquiring a rapid knowledge of Christian truth, to be the Lord's brother was a disadvantage. The physical relationship was itself fitted to make James a man of the autumn. But I think there was a second reason why the Christian life of James was retarded rather than accelerated by his growing up under the same roof with Jesus. I allude to the fact that Christianity seems in the beginning at variance with home duties. It shares this reproach in common with all poetry. Christianity is a poetic system. It professes to lift the heart into a higher and fairer world. By the man of home duties such professions are looked upon with disfavour, and, the more true they are, they are regarded with *more* disfavour. To have the heart intent on a fairer world, whether in the sphere of art or poetry or Christ, is deemed by the prosaic mind a disqualification for the things of home. Martha is always under the impression that Mary is debarred from helping her by the fact that she sits at the feet of the Master and listens to the music of another land!

Now remember, James was by nature a prosaic man; even grace did not make him otherwise. Grace never changes the distinctive sound of an instrument. It does not make the flute a violin or the trumpet a harp; what it does is to improve the quality of each instrument. James remained to the last a man of prosaic duty. His rôle was that of a practical worker, and he played that rôle to the end. But at the beginning

he thought that this rôle was incompatible
with high thinking—incompatible with poetic
flights or lofty musings or enrapturing visions.
He would have said that the man who takes
the spade in his hand should consider only the
environment of the spade and the hand—only
that soil which he is required to fructify, only
those sunbeams which he is able to utilise,
only such attributes of the wind and of the
rain as conduce to the growth of the garden.

But James lived to change his mind. How
do we know that? Because he has left us
a letter—one of the most remarkable epistles
in the New Testament, embodying the ripest
results of his Christian experience. And the
burden of that letter is a discovery which
James has made—a discovery which has
softened his whole nature. He has found
that prosaic work, home duty, humanitarian
service, so far from being at variance with
thoughts above the hour, is itself the legitimate fruit of these thoughts. 'I will show
you my faith by my works,' he cries—'I will
let you see how much better my practical

duties have been done since I entered into
the secret of Christ's pavilion and gazed upon
the vision of a brighter day.' James has here
struck upon a far-reaching principle—that the
common duties of to-day are best done by
the light of to-morrow. We see it even in
domestic service—which is God's simile for
His own service. The domestic servant has
to perform the duty of the hour; but she
will do it best if she has a hope beyond the
hour. Has she the chance of a holiday. Has
she the prospect of promotion. Has she the
promise of an increased emolument. Has she
news of some dear one coming home. Then,
even though she be jaded and languid and
weary, whatever her province may be it will
be well fulfilled—the rooms will be well swept,
the silver will be well polished, the table will
be well attended, the meal will be well prepared. Not one of us can, in moments of
fatigue and lassitude, do our work adequately
if we see nothing beyond the hour.

If you look at the letter of James in this
light, I think there will flash upon it a new

meaning and a new radiance. What, for example, is the import of that remarkable passage in the twenty-third verse of the first chapter—'If any be a hearer of the word, and not a doer, he is like unto a man beholding his natural face in a glass'? I paraphrase it thus: 'No man can do practical work by seeing his soiled face in a glass—by looking exclusively on his naturally mean aspect and squalid surroundings. That will not help you to act; it will depress you, it will paralyse you. If you want to be aided in your work, you must gaze into an ideal mirror—must see yourself, not as you are, but as you ought to be, as you may be, as you shall be. You must behold your better self, your coming self, your Godward self. You must measure your possibilities, not by viewing the marred image in the looking-glass of the past, but by contemplating the glorious form which is foreshadowed in the mirror of the future.'

This was what James had himself found by experience. He was doing the same prosaic work which he had ever done; but he was doing it much better. The reason was not that his eye was more intently fixed on the hour, but that he had come to see something beyond the hour. He had received a promise of promotion. There had opened before his vision a prospect of green fields. There had sounded in his ear a strain of far-off music. There had been wafted to his sense a perfume of sweet flowers. The vision and the music and the perfume had passed into his soul and thence into his hand. They had given a new energy to his *mind*, and that energy had streamed through his *body*. It had made him a better workman, a better servant, a better organiser. It had given him more speed, more concentration, more skill. He had found that the things of the spirit helped the things of the flesh.

Take another passage from this remarkable letter, and you will see again how James had changed his mind about the antagonism between prosaic work and ecstatic contemplation. The words to which I allude are these, 'The fervent prayer of a righteous man is powerful by its *working*.' The idea is that inward trust helps the outward hand. Let me illustrate what he means. He himself gives us a definition of what he understands by religion — 'Pure religion and undefiled before our God and Father is this, to visit the fatherless and the widows in their affliction and to keep unspotted from the world.' Now, as a mere outward act, this is a most difficult thing to do. If our view is limited to the earthly horizon, this visiting is to us a positive pain. To come into contact with scenes of misery, of poverty, of destitution, is a soul-depressing thing if one has no comfort to bring. Outside of religion, one could only continue such visiting by systematically hardening his heart. All pessimism hardens; despair is ever benumbing. And because it is benumbing, it is unfavourable to work. It may visit afflicted widows and orphans, but it will be as one visits the tombstones—with the conviction that nothing can be done. This was what James felt in the days when his heart was unsoftened. He found that he could only preach resignation, submission, sullen silence—that he could not lift by one hair-breadth the stone from the sepulchre door. But when as a Christian he began to pray, his heart was softened with hope. When there came to him an inward trust that these children of affliction were already folded in the arms of a heavenly Father who would by no means let them go until He had blessed them, then it was that James felt the impulse to action. As the ice of despair melted, the river of life began to show its possibilities. As a gleam appeared in the sky, a new energy came to the arm. He had heart to toil for these people, spirit to work for them, nerve to plan for them; the fervent trust had inspired effectual service. He felt what every sick-nurse feels — that hope is a dynamic power, that the skill of the hand is aided by the light in the heart, and that the crushing labour of to-day is shared and alleviated by the strength received from to-morrow.

James, then, through the softening contact

of Christianity, is conscious of an increased power of work. But according to this singular letter, there is another thing he is conscious of — an increased power of toleration. He says, 'The wisdom that is from above is first pure, then peaceable, gentle and easy to be intreated.' There was a time when he would have reasoned in an opposite way. He would have said, 'The wisdom from above is pure, and, because it is pure, it is uncompromising to all other systems.' What has effected the change? That the change *is* effected, is manifest. It is not only breathed in his letter; it is evinced in his life. This man whose spring was so sombre, so cold, so forbidding, is in his autumn the harbinger of peace. It is to him that we are indebted for the first oil thrown on the waters in the great controversy between the Gentile and the Jew. It is to him that we owe the decision of that peaceful Council at Jerusalem where a kindly hand was laid upon the contending parties and a conciliatory message to each healed their mutual wounds. Nay, it is to him, along

with Peter, that in the last result we attribute
the recognition by the narrow Church in
Judea of the broad apostle Paul.[1]   All this
indicates a softening of the first austerity,
an advance in the spirit of toleration.   But
whence came this advance?   Whence proceeded this increased power of toleration?
From the same source as his increased power
of work—from the spirit of Christian hope.

For, I have no hesitation in saying that
toleration as well as work is facilitated by
hope.   I know that the opposite is the common view.   The popular opinion is that intolerance is proportionate to assurance.   There
are not wanting those who say that tolerance
has advanced side by side with doubt and
that we have become less rigid as we have
become more unbelieving.   I cannot accept
this doctrine.   I believe intolerance to be
always the fruit of fear, and its opposite to be
always the fruit of confidence.   *Indifference*
may spring from unbelief; but indifference
has no more to do with toleration than with

---

[1] Gal. i. 18 and 19.

bigotry — it is the absence of all feeling. Toleration, on the other hand, implies a very profound feeling—a sense that all will be right. The tolerant man is the man who stands amid the storm and refuses by violence to suppress the winds and the waves. He is not *afraid* of the winds and the waves. The writer of the Apocalypse says of the Heavenly City, 'The gates of it shall not be shut at all by day, for there shall be no night there.' It is so with every confident human heart; nightlessness produces liberality. The heart which sees no shadow throws open its gates to all opinions. It fears not to give an entrance to sentiments not its own. Its breadth comes from its clearness, not from its cloud. Abiding faith makes abiding charity. Not from doubt, not from uncertainty, does toleration flow. It comes from a sight of the crystal river proceeding from the throne of God. The man who has entered by the door into the sheepfold has liberty to come out at pleasure and to bring pasture from other folds. The words of the

Master remain valid for all time, and cogent for all experience, 'The truth shall make you free.'

LORD, in these latter days ours is the lot of James; we are all children of the autumn. We have not seen the spring-time. We were not among those who gazed upon Thy visible glory. I have often regretted this. I have often been sad that I was 'born out of due time.' I have lamented that I have not looked upon Thy face or heard Thy voice or felt the clasp of Thy hand —that Thou hast walked in my garden only when the leaves were falling. And to me in such mood the story of Thy disciple James brings the sweetest of messages. He also was too late for the spring—too late by his own fault. Yet, spite of his lateness and spite of his blame, his autumn was bright and glorious. Thou wert at his fireside, and he saw Thee not; but he felt Thy presence when the cloud had received Thee out of his sight. I thank

Thee for that picture in the Gallery, O Lord; it speaks to *me*. It gives me hope, courage, expectation. It tells me that Thy gifts are not limited to the morning. I too may have an autumn glory. Though inland far I be, though I have never seen the ocean wave, though I hear not the water of life breaking on the shore, though the breath of the brine has passed me by and the sparkle of the spray has ignored me, I too may find Thee in the silent field. Come to my autumn, O Christ; come to my inland life! Come to the leaves that are falling; come to the woods that are thinning; come to the flowers that are fading! Bring Thine Eden to my evening, Thy Nazareth to my night! Kindle my western sky with the light of the eastern star! Speak hope to my waning years! Sing songs to my faltering feet! Plant promises in my autumn soil! Make chariots of the clouds that hide Thee! Deliver Thy beatitudes standing on the Nebo of my declining days! Then to me, as to Thy disciple, there shall be light at evening time.

12

Barnabas the Chastened

I AM now coming to the figure of a great preacher of the early Christian Church—one who in his day enjoyed the rare privilege of being the friend of opposite parties. I speak of the man who was known to his contemporaries and who is known to posterity by the name of Barnabas. The name was not his own. It was really a term of endearment meaning 'the son of consolation,' or, as it might be rendered, 'the son of exhortation.' It signified that in the opinion of men his preaching of Christian truth was of a most helpful nature, pouring balm on the wounded and giving strength to the weary. The name of love has stuck to him. It has painted him to all ages as a man of supreme kindness, of much tolerance, of wide charity—eager for the comfort of the distressed and impressed by the duties which he owed to the poor. A rich man himself, he felt that a trust had been committed to him; a preacher of Christ's Gospel, he felt that a responsibility had been laid upon him; a member of the prophetic school, he felt that he must help to hasten the march to the Promised Land.

This is the second of the great Christian preachers we have met in the Gallery. The first was John the Baptist. Nothing can exceed the difference between these two representatives of pulpit eloquence. The Baptist is immured in a Jewish desert; Barnabas grows up in the free air of Cyprus Isle and by the blue waters of a far-sounding sea. The Baptist is all fire; Barnabas is all persuasion. The Baptist would break down the stubborn strongholds; Barnabas would bind the broken hearts. The Baptist proclaims the terrors of judgment; Barnabas points to the joys of Paradise. The Baptist frightens by the famine and the swine-husks; Barnabas tempts by the ring and the robe and the welcome.

From what sin was such a good man converted?—that is the question which rises to
the lips as we gaze on his face in the Gallery.
Remember, I have no historical information
on the subject. I have never seen the primitive
Barnabas ; when he appears before me, he is
already a leader of men. Is there any other
mode of discovering his past? I think there
is. Let us look at the man as he flashes before
us in the Great Gallery at the height of his
Christian influence and in the blaze of his
Christian fame. Let us ask if even in this
white apparel we can discover the remains of
any stain, if even on this fair face we can find
the traces of a scar. If we can, you may be
sure that we have reached the *beginnings* of the
man—have put our hand on what was once
a black mark, have laid our finger on what
was originally an ugly sore.

Now, beautiful as the character of Barnabas
is, we are permitted to see in it one flaw : and
we are entitled to regard this flaw as a remaining trace of that which in the old days was
his besetting sin. What is it? I should be

disposed to describe it as a particular kind of pride—the pride of race. I say, 'a particular kind' of pride. I would sharply distinguish it, for example, from personal pride or egotism— that kind of pride to which the evangelist John in his early days was subject. The pride of race is compatible with personal humility— it may exist side by side with a sense of individual unworthiness. The Jew, indeed, was *apt* to sink himself in his country—to become personally humble in proportion as he grew patriotically proud. Again, I would distinguish this pride from the pride of wealth. Barnabas was rich, but he was not proud of his riches. In the very first recorded scene of his life we find him selling his land and giving the money to the Church. But is that incompatible with the pride of race! Would it be thought very extravagant if I said that it was the pride of race helped him to do so? Barnabas was a Levite—and the Levites, as individuals, had originally no land ; they were forbidden to inherit it, and they were at first too poor to purchase it. If, as wealth accumulated, they acquired it by purchase, a man like Barnabas might well feel that the ancestral glory had been departed from—that the law had been violated in spirit while preserved in the letter; and he might well resolve that, in his case at least, there should be a return to the life of his forefathers. I do not disparage his charity—God forbid! I do not minimise his goodness of heart—that was of the purest. But I do say that in the achieving of this good thing ancestral pride may well have co-operated, and that his personal life may have been humbled by the very consciousness of his national dignity.

Unfortunately for Barnabas, it was not always to good things that this pride led him. Perhaps I should say, 'fortunately.' A man only learns his defect in being chastened—in finding that the ways in which it leads are not ways of pleasantness nor its paths paths of peace. If it always brought him into pastures green, he might come to reverence it. But when it pushes him into quagmires, drives him among thorns, throws him down in stony places, wanders him amid labyrinths, then the man cries, 'There is something wrong here—something which incommodes me, hurts me, retards me, and which at all hazards I must get rid of.' That is the Christian history of Barnabas. It is the history of a man who has been transformed from a Jew into a follower of the Cross, but who has carried over with him a remnant of that old ancestral pride which was so prevalent among his countrymen. It is the history of that process of chastening by which this remnant of an old sin was assailed, by which the man was made to feel that the spirit of caste was not the spirit of consolation. In no other light can we read with profit the life of Barnabas. Looked at from the purely secular side, it is a very sad life. It begins in glorious morning; it closes in a cloudy afternoon. It opens with music and dancing; it concludes amid the silence. Its rise is hailed with plaudits; its setting is marked by obscurity. Very sad, I say, from a secular point of view is this life of Barnabas. But from a Christian point of view it reads

very differently. If you believe that this
decline is a chastening, if you are convinced
that the branches lopped from the tree were
useless branches, if you feel that the adversity
was a revelation that there was still something
defective in this man's soul, then will the
afternoon of Barnabas be better than his morning and the shadows of his obscurity more
healthy than the glare of his fame. Let us
briefly follow the stream of the narrative.

When the great preacher was in the blaze
of his glory, there came to Jerusalem another
and a rising preacher who promised in the
future to be great. It was young Saul of
Tarsus, who after a bitter persecution of
Christianity had been converted to the faith
he maligned and had taken the name of Paul.
There had burst upon him the conviction that
his special call was not to his own countrymen,
but to the Gentiles; it was among these that
the sun of his fame rose. From the standpoint
of the Jew this was not a very promising
beginning. That a scion of the race of Israel
should embrace a faith which professed to be

cosmopolitan, was bad enough ; that he should single out the Gentiles for a special interest, was maddening. Even the Jewish *Christians* were not prepared to hail such an advocate. They had always been accustomed to claim the largest room ; here was a man that would dispossess them of their privilege ! Might not this be only another form of the persecution— an attempt to destroy Christ by denying His special relation to the land of their fathers ! Was this a man to be trusted ! Were his antecedents such as made him an object of trust ! Had he not been a bitter enemy of their faith ! Was a change so sudden as his likely to be real, or, if real, likely to be permanent ! Were they not standing on the brink of a precipice ; let them beware !

And so, when this young preacher came to Jerusalem, he was received coldly. Men shrank from him as from a pestilence. There are times when nothing can raise a man in public estimation but the support of a powerful hand. The man who is under disgrace, under suspicion, under the ban of the multitude, will probably lie there until he is lifted by some one higher than the multitude. But when that happens, the influence of the one will in all likelihood outweigh the influence of the many. So was it with Paul. For a time he lay prostrate in obscurity—shunned and feared by his Christian countrymen. Suddenly, a big hand touched him, and two big arms lifted him up, and a big voice proclaimed, 'This man is our brother.' The hand, the arms, the voice, were those of Barnabas. It was exactly the thing we should expect Barnabas to do. He was by nature a consoler. The sounds which first reached his ear were ever the plaints of weakness. To be downtrodden, to have everybody against you, to be despised and rejected by your fellow-men, was quite sufficient to place you within sight of the sympathy of Barnabas. His large heart took in the desolate Paul and made a way for him in the world. He led him to the College of Apostles. He brought him to the President of that college—James the Lord's brother, to win whose influence was the key to the whole position. He

told of Paul's zeal, of his ardour, of his success.
He lost no opportunity of bringing his talents
into notice. When Paul had gone back to
Tarsus and Barnabas had gone to electrify
with his wisdom the Church at Antioch, the
older preacher was sad because he had all the
glory. He wanted the young man to share
it; he determined that he should share it. He
went to Tarsus and brought him to the scene
of triumph. He gave him a place among the
Christian workers. He went about continually
in his company, that men might say, 'There
go Barnabas and Paul.' He knew well the
power of association—how a tarnished name
if linked with a great name may lose its
tarnish; and he resolved that Paul should
reap the advantage of such a union.

This was generous, this was noble. But
what if the association should be inverted!
What if in process of time the conjunction
should be, not 'Barnabas and Paul,' but 'Paul
and Barnabas'! It is quite a common thing
to see a mature preacher take a young preacher
under his patronage, and in a brief space to

behold the young man becoming the leader. In the present instance this actually happened. For a while the name of Barnabas precedes, and that of Paul follows; then there is a change—the order is 'Paul and Barnabas.' The reason is plain. Paul has revealed himself as the greater power. I do not say, as the greater *man*. If Christian greatness be the spirit of goodness, Barnabas must ever remain one of the loftiest human souls. But if Barnabas was unsurpassed as a man, he was surpassed as a power. It was not long before a superior force made itself felt in the little band—it was the mind of Saul of Tarsus. He entered as a dependent; he ended as a leader. He came to the front by the sheer force of intellect. His mind was in some respects a contrast to that of Barnabas. Barnabas was entirely practical; Paul was, before all things, speculative. Barnabas was naturally calm; Paul was generally on fire. Barnabas was methodical; Paul moved on wings. Barnabas was an organiser; Paul was an inspirer. Barnabas was a man of counsel; Paul was a man of genius. It was inevitable that the stronger force should in the long-run be the dominant force; it was certain from the outset that the leading spirit of the company would be, not Barnabas, but Paul.

But the question which I ask is this, What effect would this have upon Barnabas? Would it touch his jealousy? Never—that, at least, may be confidently affirmed. This man was incapable of jealousy. It had no part in his nature, which was essentially free from individual self-seeking. But if you ask me if it would touch his pride of race, then, looking to what happened afterwards, I must give a very different answer. I think this is the very element in Barnabas which the superior deference paid to Paul would touch. It is true, Paul was as Jewish as himself and had a lineage as good as his own. But those of whom Paul was exclusively the missionary were, in the view of Barnabas, without lineage—the Gentiles had no descent from Abraham. Why should one who represented the Gentiles alone, be seated on a higher throne than one who, however tolerant and however eager to make Gentile converts, had been originally the representative of an older and more venerable line—of that Church which professed to be the latest flower of Judaism and the fulfilment of her Messianic dreams! Was it right, was it well, that it should be so! Ought not the first branch to be the cherished branch! Had it not been deemed in days of yore the proudest of all dignities to belong to the primitive fold; why had the time come when men were turning aside from this reverence to crown one who served the fold of a stranger!

I think that, parallel with his own declining influence, this was the ever-deepening thought of Barnabas. It was not a jealous feeling, it was not even a personal feeling; it was the pride of race. He thought of himself, not as an individual, but as the member of a venerable community which, in the mind even of the Gentile, should ever have the highest place of reverence. Yet, impersonal as it was, the feeling was the remnant of a garment which ought to have been discarded, and which, because it was not discarded, became a source of discord. It was not long before the cloud brooding over the heart was made visible in the sky. It first gathered at Perga. John Mark, the favourite nephew of Barnabas, deserted the Gentile band and went back to the Mother Church at Jerusalem. In the next chapter I shall speak of him separately, and I only allude to him now with a view to illustrate the attitude of Barnabas. But I think his conduct has a bearing on the attitude of Barnabas. When I remember that even after the separation the uncle and nephew still remained on excellent terms, when I recollect how amply it was revealed in the future that the elder man had condoned the deed of the younger, I cannot avoid the conclusion that in the mind of that elder man there had risen a shadow of displeasure which had dimmed the glory of the morning and spread a chill through the once-genial air.

But the shadow was to deepen, the chill

was to increase. By and by there was a con-
ference summoned at Antioch.[1] It was to be
a meeting for purposes of Church-union. All
parties were to be represented; all parties
came. The *Gentile* Christians were probably
first in the field—Antioch being a Gentile city.
Then would come the Hellenists—the men
who, though now Grecianised, had either been
originally pure Jews or had sprung from
Jewish ancestors; and these sat down beside
the purely Gentile converts. Then appeared
the *Jewish* Christians; and they too sat down
with the Hellenist and the Jew. At last came
deputies from that ecclesiastical board of ad-
ministration over which James presided—men
who, however liberal, were full of Jewish
memories and deep in the caste of nationality. And when these came, they would not
sit down with the mass. They were willing
to make copious *concessions* to the Gentiles,
but not to give their company; they could
patronise, but not fraternise. They held themselves apart. They kept in an isolated corner.

---

[1] So I interpret Galatians ii. 11-14.

They constituted themselves an inner court of the tabernacle and allowed the party of Paul to remain outside. Gradually, an effect was produced by this attitude. The Jewish Christians began to steal away from the seats they had taken and to form independent groups. Peter quietly removed himself—but simply from a return of his native timidity. There was worse to follow—*Barnabas* removed himself. This was not timidity, nor was it the impulse of the hour. It must have been the result of a long process of dissatisfaction. Barnabas was not an impulsive man and he was not a passionate man. What he did he did from reflection—a reflection which, though bitter, was dictated, I believe, by an erroneous sense of duty. I think it was really at *him* that Paul levelled his rebuke. He addressed Peter, but only because he was the virtual chairman of the company. It was Barnabas that made him sore. It was Barnabas that awakened his astonishment and indignation. It was Barnabas that quickened him to the frailty of human nature and to the inveterate and wellnigh invincible weakness that dwells in the heart of man.

At last the cloud descended in a stream of piteous rain. In process of time Paul proposed that he and Barnabas should make a second missionary tour over the ground they had already trodden. Barnabas, you will observe, has now ceased to be the suggester of the Gospel programme; its ordering has passed into the hand of Paul. Yet the former leader is willing here to be the follower. He consents to go, provided Paul will allow John Mark to accompany them. Paul emphatically refuses. Had not this man deserted the standard! Had he not preferred another field to the field so dear to Paul's heart! Were any family considerations to alleviate the blame of such conduct! John Mark must be viewed, not as the nephew of Barnabas, but as a neutral party! He must be treated on his own merits—not as the scion of an old house, but as if he were an individual unbefriended, obscure, alone! Judged by that test, he had been found wanting! There was a rent in his garment which could not be patched over with family colours; let the man abide where he had elected to be. So said Paul; and it was the last straw. For then the storm broke. Barnabas retorted; Paul replied. The waters pent up for months burst their barriers and rushed into the open. The quarrel which began with being vicarious became personal; mutual recriminations came, and words ran high. At last that happened which in such cases often happens—the less capable combatant left the room and slammed the door. That was in effect what Barnabas did. He threw up his work. He abandoned the mission. He bade farewell to the scene of his labours, to Paul, to the comrades of his midday. He withdrew into his shell—Cyprus. He saw the drama of a great career fade before him; and his life which promised to fill the world was confined within the limits of a little isle. There was again a change in the Gospel partnership. First it had been 'Barnabas and Paul'; then it was 'Paul and Barnabas'; henceforth it was to be ' Paul' alone.

Who was wrong in the *result* of this quarrel?
Undoubtedly Barnabas. I waive altogether
the subject of John Mark's treatment. It is
a question which is irrelevant; and it ought to
have been a question subordinate to Gospel
interests. Why should Barnabas have allowed
a family consideration to outweigh his work for
Christ! Why should he have diminished that
work for any discourtesy paid to his house! I
believe this last act of his was a final judgment on that lingering weakness of his life—
the pride of race. I feel sure that before long
it was accepted as such by himself—as his
revelation of the pitfall in the way. Why do
I think that he lived to regret the step he
had taken? So far as I know, he and Paul
never met again; what makes me think that
Barnabas came to shake hands in spirit?
There are two things which lead me to that
conclusion. One is the fact that, long years
afterwards, an extravagantly Pauline letter
appeared bearing the name of Barnabas. Its
genuineness is outwardly very well attested;
internally, the production is thought very un-

like him. The reason of the supposed unlike-
ness is just the fact that he is so unfettered
in his treatment of the Jewish scriptures—one
would say he had passed over to the Gentiles.
Altogether, I do not myself think that he is
the author of that letter ; but I do think that
the fact of its being attributed to him shows
where, in his last years, his mind was known
to lie. It shows that in the opinion of his
contemporaries his life, as it neared the setting
sun, came nearer and ever nearer to that
ocean of universal love in which Paul bathed
all the day—where there was neither Jew nor
Greek, barbarian nor Roman, bond nor free—
where the only flag unfurled was the flag of
humanity.

But there is another reason why I think
the closing years of Barnabas were years of
reconciliation. The nephew came back to
Paul—came back under circumstances which
made the sacrifice all on his side and the gain
entirely on Paul's. As the subject will recur
hereafter I shall not dwell upon it here. The
one point is that the nephew did come back—

came back at a time when love alone could
have brought him. And when we consider that
after Paul had rejected his services he had gone
to live with his uncle, his act of reconciliation
throws back its light upon Barnabas. It shows
clearly that the spirit of Barnabas had been
sweetened by the years. If the impression
left by the uncle on the nephew's mind had
been one of bitterness, he would have shunned
Paul for evermore. We do not love those
by whom a near and dear relative has been
stung, even where the sting has been justly
implanted. The return of John Mark proves
to my mind that from the breast of Barnabas
the sting had been long extracted, and that
in its room had been planted the spirit of
reconciliation. It proves that, in his sphere
of comparative imprisonment in the isle of
Cyprus, the *heart* of Barnabas, at least, had
burst its chain. Though no longer he was
aiding Paul with the hand, his soul was going
with him. His sympathies were breaking forth
from Cyprus and following his companion of
early years—rejoicing in his triumphs, sharing

in his griefs, participating in his burdens, joining in his prayers. The outward union to him personally was not to be restored; but the union in the spirit was already complete, and to his kinsman he left the clasping of the hands.

L ORD, let not the sun go down upon my wrath! Life is too short for quarrels. Yet it is not because life is short that I would have peace. It is because eternity is long. How strange my old quarrels look in the light of vanished years! Methinks they will look stranger still in the light of Thine eternity. I am ambitious now, and I shall be ambitious then; but the things for which I am ambitious now are not the things for which I shall be ambitious then. Now I strive to get; then I shall strive to give. Now I seek possession; then I shall try to be dispossessed. Now I covet the uppermost seat; then I shall descend the stair. Now I select the best robe; then I shall choose the

servant's form. I see Paul and Barnabas
standing before Thy presence, and there is
still a strife between them. But the cause
of strife is changed—Paul wishes Barnabas
to be first, and Barnabas is eager to remain
second; they *wonder* at their old quarrel in
the light of Thy throne. Reveal that light
to me, O Lord! In my hour of quarrel, in
the hour when I strive to be first, give me
a glimpse of the soul's last judgment on
itself—its reversed judgment! Let me see
Cain rejoicing over the acceptance of Abel's
sacrifice! Let me see Lot repudiating the
richer share! Let me see Sarah making a
home for Ishmael! Let me see Jacob refusing his brother's birthright! Let me see
Joseph exalting his brethren in his dreams!
Let me see David take Uriah's place in the
battle! Let me see Jonah intent on sparing
Nineveh! Let me see Herod exulting in the
sustenance of the babes of Bethlehem! Then
shall the light of eternity arrest the strife of
time; Paul and Barnabas shall stand side
by side.

13

Mark the Steadied

ON that night in which Jesus was betrayed, all who were with Him in the Garden forsook Him and fled. But there was one who followed Him though he had *not* been with Him in the Garden. When the soldiers came out to the public road leading their august prisoner, an obscure young man did what the others had feared to do—took a few steps in company with Jesus. It was only a few steps—his strength was not equal to the strain; when the soldiers laid hands upon his garment he *left* it in their hands and fled like the rest. Yet he had gone a yard or two further than the men of the Garden in the following of Jesus. He had at least made a movement forward, not backward; and, by that short walk, 'he, being dead, yet speaketh.'

I doubt not that the recording angel wrote
down his name, or rather his namelessness,
as a proof that the obscure may often sur-
pass the illustrious, and that he expressed
the sense of his superiority to the watchers in
the Garden by affixing the inscription, 'A day's
march nearer home.'

Now, in the view of tradition this young
man was Mark the Evangelist. It is in his
Gospel the story is told, and he has been
thought by many to be speaking of himself.
Let it be understood, once for all, that when
I say 'Mark the Evangelist' I mean every
man who in the New Testament is mentioned
by the name of Mark—whether it be John
Mark or the Mark whom Paul summons to
Rome or the Mark who resides with Peter in
Babylon. I prejudge no question of criticism
as to matters of fact. But when the question
is simply, What is meant to be conveyed by
the artist? I have no hesitation in accepting
the belief that in the design of the Gallery
they are all one and the same person. My
whole province here is to expound the Gallery.

I shall start therefore with the assumption that in the Gallery of the New Testament there is but one figure of the name—a figure which passes through a variety of changes in its transition from youth to maturity—which rises in the heart of Jerusalem and is lost to view in the heart of Rome—which is known to its contemporaries as the nephew of Barnabas and to all posterity as the writer of a Gospel. We shall endeavour to weave into unity these various threads which at first seem separate and independent, and to present the picture of this man as the representative of a distinct idea and the embodiment of a special thought.

Whether John Mark be or be not the young man described at the egress from the Garden, there can be no doubt that the description suits him. We see there the picture of a splendid advance and a sudden recoil. That is exactly the portrait of Mark. If I were asked to indicate his leading feature, I should define him as 'the unsteady man.' Let me explain precisely what I mean. It is quite

a common thing among ourselves to say of a
young man, ' Unfortunately, he is not steady.'
But when we say that, we always imply one
thing—that he is not steady in well-doing.
We generally apply the phrase to one who,
after walking awhile in pastures green, is found
staggering with drink in street and lane. That
is certainly an interruption of steadiness; but
it is not the unsteadiness of which I here
speak, nor that which I attribute to John
Mark. In the broad and strict sense of the
word, unsteadiness has no more to do with
ill-doing than with well-doing. An unsteady
young man is a young man who is unable to
keep to one definite purpose—who in a brief
space deserts it for another. So far as this
quality is concerned, it matters nothing whether
he wavers between the good and the bad,
between the bad and the bad, or between
the good and the good ; each of these cases
alike implies an irresolute will. Many a man
turns from one occupation to another with
perfect honesty and perfect conviction. He
may begin by trying to write history ; then

he may attempt science; then he may aspire to poetry; then he may take up the work of the artist. We call such an unsteady man. Not one of the conflicting aims is bad—they are each good and noble. But the fact that in the man's mind they *are* conflicting, proves him to be unsteady. I do not think that John Mark ever deserted a good cause for a bad; the point is that he was constantly deserting one cause for another. This is why I call him 'Mark the unsteady.' He stands as a representative of the man who does not know his own mind, the unstable man, the wavering man. His impulses are all for good; but they are not long directed toward the same good; it is the blue to-day, the green to-morrow, the red next day. He never sinks to the degraded; but he has no permanent interest in any particular cause which is sublime.

When we first meet the name of John Mark, he is already a Christian. He was in an admirable atmosphere for becoming a Christian. He belonged to a Christian family. His uncle was Barnabas. His mother was Mary of Jerusalem—a woman of worldly means and unworldly piety. Her house in the Jewish metropolis was a place of rendezvous—a salon where met from time to time the leaders of the faith. Sometimes it was for purposes of prayer, sometimes for exhortation, sometimes for social intercourse. Amid the amenities of this circle young Mark enjoyed great advantages; he learned the nature of Christianity almost from the fountainhead, and he saw it represented in its adaptation to varied minds. The man whom he first met was the man who bound the earliest cord round his heart; it was Simon Peter. The Master had given to Peter the key to many human doors; and the door of Mark's spirit opened to him of its own accord. There was something in the natures of these men which drew them into harmony. They had both naturally the same mental disease—a wavering will. The causes of the malady were of course very different. Peter was originally timid and was frightened by the first cloud; Mark was constitutionally volatile and was drawn elsewhere by the second sunbeam. Yet the fact of a common disease made a common sympathy, while the difference of its cause created a power of mutual help. If the wavering in each case had come from the same source, Peter and Mark might have been sympathisers; but they never could have been helpers, for mutual help demands that each should possess an element which is lacking in the other. The blended likeness and difference of these men united them on two sides.

Then, by and by, there came to Jerusalem the man who was to become the other figure of the apostolic age—Paul of Tarsus. He was brought by Barnabas as a fellow-worker in the relieving of a great famine. Here Mark for the first time met Paul. I do not think the man of Tarsus made as much impression upon him as Peter had done. There was little resemblance in their characters. If Mark was wavering, Paul was inflexible. If Mark had many objects of attraction, Paul had only one. If Mark was drawn aside by passing

sentiment, Paul was bound by the chain of a
permanent love. Nor do I think that at this
stage the cause of Paul was the cause of Mark.
I believe that originally the heart of the latter
was not with the Gentiles, but with the Jews.
It is not often that the younger generation is
less liberal than the older ; but I think Mark
was far more conservative than his uncle
Barnabas. They had lived in a different
environment. Barnabas had dwelt in the
comparatively free air of Cyprus, and had
seen many phases of many minds. He was
in the position of the man of travel. He had
come to find that there must be allowed a
certain amount of latitude for human thought,
and that we cannot expect all men to be
shaped in one mould. Mark, on the other
hand, was a child of Jerusalem. With Jerusalem were linked his earliest, and therefore
his fondest, associations. It was the home
of his happiest years, the scene of his most
cherished memories. Religion itself had come
to him there, and had come in a joyous dress
—wreathed with social interest and decked

with colours gay. Jerusalem was very dear to Mark, and anything that disparaged her, anything that would tend to put her in the second place, must have been strongly distasteful to him. The enthusiasm for the Gentile world was not to him the most joyful of sounds.

Nevertheless, Barnabas requested that his nephew should accompany him in his missionary tour with Paul I think the proposal came from Barnabas. I think he was afraid that the young man was getting inured to a narrow atmosphere. If *Paul* had made the request it is probable it would have been refused. But when it came from the uncle, when it was dictated by solicitude for Mark's mental enlargement, when it was an appeal for companionship by one for whom he cherished an affection and who cherished an affection for him, it spoke to impulses outside of religion and impulses which were fitted to strike the youthful mind. Mark said, ' I will go.'

Accordingly, when Paul and Barnabas departed from Jerusalem they took Mark with

them. It was a very unpromising beginning
for a missionary career. No man should enter
on such a career with any motive less than zeal
for the cause. Every step of Mark's journey
increased his homesick longing for the Christian Church of Jerusalem. I know that his dis-
content has been attributed to lower motives.
Men have spoken of him as lazy, idle, somnolent, unwilling to put his hand to the plough
lest it should be soiled, averse to expose his
life lest it should be sacrificed. A more
ungenerous verdict was never pronounced—
it is refuted by his whole life. Mark was not
a selfish man ; he was never an idle man ; in
his later years he was the reverse of a timid
man—and these are the only years when he
had a real chance of displaying himself. His
bane was that he was a man of two ideas—
not of one. His was not a struggle between
the love of action and the love of ease. It
was a struggle with the temptation to act in
different ways either of which would in itself
be good. It was in the present instance a
struggle whether to abide with Paul or to

return to Peter. A man of steady will would have battled down the temptation to return. But Jerusalem the Golden, the Jerusalem of his youth, the Jerusalem of his earliest joys, was too strong for him; it kept a corner in his heart and would not let him go.

So, when the little company arrived at Perga, Mark suddenly disappeared. I know not in what manner he effected his departure—whether he simply abandoned them or made an excuse for absence or wrote a respectful letter of resignation. It may be safely said that nothing could confer dignity on his departure. Paul could only receive it as a slight to the cause which was dearest to his heart—a slight all the more impressive and all the more stinging because it came from the nephew of the very man who had been his patron in the hour of need; it was apt to make men say, 'If Paul's own friends desert him, we need not wonder at what his enemies do.' Mark went back to Jerusalem. He was probably received with contempt—as a rolling stone. A rolling stone he certainly was; but it was not rolling downhill. His was really a case of religious homesickness. He was attached to the Church of his fathers. Their city was to him the sacred city, their temple the model and pattern of the house of God. His heart could not beat in unison with a movement which centred round other cities and bowed the knee at other shrines. He was jealous for the place of his birth, for the school of his religious training, for the associations and memories of his youth; and he was unwilling to bear a part in the injuring of these. There was an element of true loyalty in the weakness of John Mark.

By and by something happened at Jerusalem which modified Mark's view. A conciliatory council was held there to soften the differences between Jews and Gentiles. As the result of that council the Church at Jerusalem gave a patronising recognition to the Gentiles. Phlegmatic and unaccompanied with enthusiasm as the recognition was, it suggested to Mark the possibility of another rolling movement on his part. Was not Paul put in a new light by this act of the council! Had not the Mother

Church taken him under her wing! Had not Jerusalem given him her blessing! Could not Mark now offer his services to Paul *without* being disloyal to Jerusalem! On the former occasion he had felt like a traitor to the past; but surely that reproach could not exist now! Might he not go back to Paul and say, 'My Church has publicly recognised the rights of the Gentiles; I may with a clear conscience return to *you*'! And then, his uncle Barnabas was pleading with him to come back. He missed the nephew's company. His relations with Paul had become somewhat strained. He had begun to feel alone and unbefriended. He wanted a kinsman—some one to whom he could pour out his heart. When Mark considered all these things he was disposed to return. He allowed Barnabas to make the proposal to Paul. But Paul refused to receive him—and from his point of view he may be excused in so doing. His strong and inflexible nature could not respect rolling stones. He was unwilling to admit into his band of workers a weak and wavering soul. Mark had recently deserted his cause; why in so brief a space should he change his mind again! Was such a rapid reconversion any compliment to that cause, or did it give any security for permanent adherence! Would not the enrolling of such a man be only the introducing into the ranks of an element of weakness and the sowing of unpromising seed in a healthy and fertile field!

But if the modern spectator can excuse Paul, Barnabas could not; he threw up the cause and retired to Cyprus. He did not go alone. He asked Mark to accompany him—which shows that his wish to bring him back had been rather personal than ecclesiastical. And here the unfortunate Mark again changes his front. He goes to Cyprus. He had been a Jew; he had been a Jewish Christian; he had been a Gentile Christian; he had been a Jewish Christian once more; he was well-nigh becoming a Gentile Christian once more. Thwarted in this last resolve, what does he become now? What name should we give to him in Cyprus? I would call him the companion to

a good man. I think he went neither for Jew
nor Gentile, but purely for the sake of Barnabas.
I have heard men sneer at this mission to
Cyprus. I have seen Christian writers point
with scorn to the narrow sphere he had chosen
for his labours and the life of laziness he had
purchased for his soul. It is an ungenerous
sneer. The mission of Mark to Cyprus was
not a religious mission. It was a mission of
human sympathy — sympathy for a private
friend. He went to comfort the grief and
cheer the solitude of one who had always
loved and befriended him and whose very
sorrow had been incurred in the effort to do
him service. You may call his journey to
Cyprus another movement of the stone ; yet it
was a movement not toward worldly pleasure
but toward Christian sacrifice.

How long Mark remained in Cyprus I do
not know—it may have been for years. In
any case, it must have been a time of much
benefit, moral and intellectual. He met the
Gentiles in a field where there was no conflict
—the life of social intercourse. He was able

to look at them as men and women bearing a common burden — to view them as fellow-citizens apart from creed, apart from sect, apart from church-membership, and to feel that the soul of man was larger than his systems. I doubt not that the days of Mark in Cyprus did him good.

But there was coming to this man a greater good still — an event which was to be the turning-point of his life. There came to him one day a call from across the sea ; and the voice that uttered it was that of the man who had attracted his youthful years—Simon Peter. He called on Mark to help him—not as a missionary, but as a secretary. The former fisherman of Galilee knew well the advantage he would reap from superior culture. He knew that Mark had received that culture — that he had possessed from youth all the opportunities which wealth can bring. There had been no hindrance to his education. He had enjoyed the influences of social refinement and the amenities of a happy home. He had not been tossed upon the sea as he himself had been, but had been allowed to pitch his tent upon the hill. His superior leisure had given him superior learning. Peter wanted such a man—one who could clothe his thoughts and interpret them to the people. Mark heard his cry for help, and he said, ' I will go.' Barnabas himself must have urged him to go. All through his life no such suitable opening had appeared for John Mark. It was a place made for him, cut out for him, fitted to bring into bold relief all that was best and truest and noblest within him, and to waken that which had long been asleep in his heart—a definite purpose in living.

Little did John Mark know where in this new occupation his opening was to lie. It was not in having a fixed profession. It was not in being thrown into direct contact with the apostles. It was not even in the companionship with so great a soul as Peter. It was in a greater companionship—that of Christ Himself. Mark received from Peter the notes of a Gospel. When he put these together there emerged a portrait of the

Master—the first portrait of the Master that was ever presented to the human eye. As Mark gazed upon the unexpected result of his own handiwork, his spirit was stirred within him. What did he see? The one thing he needed to see — an aim in life. Hitherto he had wavered between Jew and Gentile. As he looked into that face, Jew and Gentile alike vanished, and there shone out only one form—Man. Jerusalem faded; Antioch faded; and over the blank spaces there rose the republic of human souls. As he gazed upon that portrait there dawned on him a great thought—the idea that what gave men equal rights was neither Judaism nor Gentilism, but the common cross of humanity. What was that earliest portrait of the Master which we now call the Gospel of Mark? It was the picture which delineated a great physician—a healer of human woes. It was the portrait of a soul that had put deeds in the place of words — that felt life was too short for verbal controversy and must be approached by the work of the hand. It was the depicting of one who did not ask at the outset, 'Are you a Jew?' 'Are you a Gentile?' 'Are you a worshipper of any kind?' but whose primary question was, 'Have you anything requiring to be healed?'

And this portrait woke Mark's soul. There rose within him a great resolve—he would *follow* that picture of the Master. He would stand aside in the question between Gentile and Jew; he would devote himself to a larger problem. He would become a sick-nurse to humanity, a minister to human need. And by and by there occurred a chance for testing his resolve. His old antagonist Paul came to the depths of sorrow. His splendid missionary career was at last interrupted; the bird was arrested in its flight, and caged. The apostle, trapped by his Jewish countrymen, languished within a prison at Cæsarea. A thought comes to Mark. Was not this the place in which the definite purpose of his life should begin! Could there be a better time for indecision to vanish and wavering to cease! He had determined to follow the healing footsteps of Jesus; were they not leading him first of all to Cæsarea to help his opponent of former days! Paul had doubted the genuineness of his Gentilism; would he doubt the genuineness of his humanity! If he went to him in his poverty, in his loneliness, in his hour of enforced inaction—if he brought wealth to supply his needs, fellowship to meet his solitude, a ministrant hand to assist his weariness—would not Paul at last believe in him! Mark resolves that he will yield to Paul's adversity the homage which he had refused to his prosperity, and that he will lend to his hours of weakness the service of a slave to his master.

We know how gloriously his promise was fulfilled; there was no faltering, no paltering, no altering, any more. He came to the prison at Cæsarea and supplicated permission to serve. I know not how Paul received him. Perhaps at first the gifts appeared anonymously—Paul may have been *beguiled* into love. But I know that ere long he was conscious of Mark's nobleness—conscious that at last a steady race had begun. Almost the latest act of his life was to look back on these days at Cæsarea, and record his sense of how profitable this man's ministration had been. He gives him his word of recommendation—he asks the Church to receive him. Nay, there is something more touching still. When the apostle's last day is drawing near, when death stares him in the face, when most of the companions of his former years have fled, who is it that he asks for, who is it that he longs to see? It is Mark. I can imagine no greater compliment paid by man to man. I should think it worth while to be rejected a hundred times if as a recompense I received such an approach at last. Did Mark go? I feel sure he did. I have no doubt that he went with Timothy to Rome to cheer Paul's latest hours; and I believe that he remained there to lead the ambulance corps of humanity. There, not inappropriately, we shall leave him—in the city of the steadfast, in the place where of all others men had learned the wisdom of inflexible tenacity. That city will confirm him in his acquired robustness, and he will impart to her somewhat of his original softness ; and it may be that from this union there shall at length emerge a beautiful and harmonious blend.

L ORD, I should like to join the ambulance corps of humanity. I would rather be a member of that band than either a Gentile or a Jew. Thou art leading our age where Mark was led—to the bearing of the cross. Never has Thy portrait been studied so deeply as now. In past days we studied other portraits, and therefore we aspired to other things than the human. We gazed on Paul and cried, 'Great is the mystery of Godhead!' We gazed on Peter and said, 'Show us the things which the *angels* desire to look into!' We gazed on John and exclaimed, 'Let us see the city of gold!' We gazed on Matthew and breathed the prayer, 'Unroll the book of prophecy!'

These were aspirings after *heaven*. But it is only now that we have begun to aspire after earth, have desired to see *its* mysteries unveiled. It is only in gazing into *Thy* face that we have seen the face of our brother-man. Thou hast kept the best wine till the last, O Lord. I had been long seeking to pierce the clouds of nature, but I had never pierced the cloud in my brother's soul—never till I saw *Thee*. Now there has come to me a new evangel, nay, the old misread evangel. Thou hast said to my soul, 'Why standest thou gazing up into heaven! the Son of Man is coming down from heaven to earth.' I asked Thee to open the sky; Thou hast said, 'Open the prison doors!' I asked Thee for a tabernacle on the mount; Thou hast said, 'Heal the demoniac on the plain!' I asked Thee for a sign of Thy coming; Thou hast said, 'It will be man's humanity to man.' I asked Thee how I should learn Thy doctrine; Thou hast said, 'Feed my sheep!' I asked for a gate into the temple; Thou hast pointed to a door in the hospital. I asked for Thy robing-room ; Thou hast shown me an orphanage home. I asked to drink of Thy cup ; Thou hast sent me to scenes of misery. I asked to share Thy glory ; Thou hast called me to restore one fallen soul. The service to my Father has become the service to my brother ; give me a place, O Lord, in earth's ambulance corps !

14

Cornelius the Transplanted

IT may seem strange that I should place the name of Cornelius after those of Barnabas and Mark. Cornelius only figures at the dawn of the apostolic age, Barnabas and Mark survive into its midday; why fall back from a later to an earlier life? It is because in these pages I have followed a definite principle of chronology. I have placed first in order of time those figures of the Gallery which came into clear and undoubted contact with the earthly life of the Master—Peter, John, Thomas, and the like. Next in order of time I have placed the two men whose contact with the earthly Christ is doubtful—Barnabas and Mark. The former is said to have been one of the seventy to whom Christ personally intrusted a mission; the latter, as

I have already stated, has been traditionally
identified with the young man who followed
Jesus from the Garden. These, however, are
matters of conjecture, and so I have given
to the subjects of them a later place. After
these I have put those who neither in history
nor in tradition have been enrolled amid the
band which in His human form beheld the
Lord. Foremost among these in point of
time is the man Cornelius. He is not a
Jewish figure; he is not even an Eastern
figure. He is a man of the West, a European,
a Roman. He is not only separated from
outward contact with *Jesus*; he is separated
from outward contact with the environment
of Jesus. His life has been spent in war—
in the service of an empire whose aims
were *not* Messianic. He had breathed the
atmosphere of the camp rather than the air
of Calvary, had heard, not sermons on the
mount, but ribald jests on the highway.
Cornelius was the child of an empire which
had passed its meridian glory—the empire of
Tiberius, the empire of Caligula, the empire

which had lost the form of sound words and the semblance of good deeds. He had not been born within the compass of church bells.

By and by this man, as the captain of a regiment, was ordered to Cæsarea. He was sent there to represent the fact of Roman conquest, to exercise a military surveillance over the district. But, all the time that he was keeping military watch over Judea, Judea kept moral watch over him. He came to represent Rome's conquest of Israel; he ended by representing Israel's conquest of Rome. He was converted by his own dependents— converted to the faith of Judaism. His nature became transformed. The dissolute man grew devout. The proud man became prayerful. The grasping man began to lavish gratuities. The undomesticated man took up the duties of a household, and specially the care of its religious life. Cornelius was conquered by the moral power of Judaism. There are souls that in their ascent to Christianity pass first through the faith of their ancestors. Cornelius was one of these.

He began as a Pagan, the worshipper of many gods. Then he rose to be a Jew, the worshipper of one God of righteousness. Another step remained to make him perfect; he had to become a Christian, the worshipper of a God of grace.

We are disposed, indeed, to wonder what was lacking to Cornelius. His Jewish faith is described in such glowing colours that we are tempted to ask what more could be desired. A man of devoutness, a man of prayer, a man of domestic virtue, a man of public charity—has he not already done everything which a Christian can do! Perhaps. A boy who has been through the school methods of arithmetic can do everything in matters of calculation that an office-clerk can do. But he will not do it in the same manner, nor with the same quickness, and therefore he could not be an office-clerk. Before he can become that, he must get rid of his school method, and learn a short road to the goal. The most perfect penmanship will not fit a man to be a reporter. In process of time he could by ordinary penmanship do all that the reporter does ; but the process of time is just what is denied to him ; there is required a shorthand process. That is what Cornelius needed. He could calculate splendidly, he could write beautifully ; but he could do both only by school methods. He wanted a means of coming to the goal with more ease and with more rapidity—of reaching the summit of the hill, not by an act of laborious climbing, but by the movement of an eagle's wing. This was the new stage that was coming to Cornelius.

The strange thing is that in teaching Cornelius His own new evangel, God is represented in this picture as following the old-school method. The man is to be taught a quick way of reaching heaven ; but he is taught it in a most cumbrous, lengthy, and laborious manner. Have you ever considered the singular character of that picture in the tenth chapter of Acts. The man Cornelius is about to receive the Holy Spirit—the most unfettered gift which the Divine can bestow upon the human. Why does it not come unfettered to Cornelius? We should expect that it would have rushed into his soul like a flash of sunshine, like a breath of morning. Does it? Listen to the lengthened process! There comes to him a shining angel and tells him that he is under the favour of heaven. He bids Cornelius send men to Joppa to summon Simon Peter, and gives directions for finding his lodging. Three men are sent on a day's journey to invite the apostle to Joppa — two domestics of Cornelius and a soldier who waited on him. One would think the Divine would have quicker modes of telegraphy! In the meantime, Peter also is prepared by a vision for the receiving of a Gentile convert, is told to count nothing common or unclean. One asks, What need of this preparation — ought he not to have known that in the seed of Abraham all nations were to be blessed! Then Peter is wakened from his dream by a knocking at the door, and the three messengers of Cornelius enter. They tell their story, and abide the whole day.

Next morning they set out for Cæsarea, accompanied by Peter and a retinue of his fellow-Christians; and it is the following day before they arrive. Cornelius, too, has gathered to meet Peter a company of his kinsmen. He falls down before the apostle in an attitude of worship—showing that the Paganism was not quite dead in his nature. Peter raises him up and bids him transfer his homage to Jesus. Then follows a sermon on the life and work of Jesus; and, as the words strike the ear, the gift of God at last descends, and Cornelius and his whole company are filled with the Holy Ghost.

Now, to what purpose is this waste! Why extend over three days an act that might have been momentary! Why use so much machinery for a deed that might have been spontaneous! The Divine Spirit required no human message to Joppa — much less three messengers. Simon Peter could not bring Cornelius one step nearer to God Almighty; he was already as near as he could be without touching Him. Why revert to the

stage-coach when we have the railway-train!
The Spirit's province is to blow where it listeth
—as the lightning cometh out of the east and
shineth even unto the west. There must be
some *cause* for this choice of a long way. If
an object is within reach of your hand and
you ring a bell to call from the other end of
the house some one who will give it to you,
it is clear you must have a motive beyond the
acquiring of the object. Can we discover any
motive for the use of so many hands in the
conversion of one man?

I think we can. Remember who this one
man is. He is a soldier. The design of this
picture is to delineate the transplanting of a
soldier. I say, 'the transplanting.' Cornelius
is not to be annihilated and created a new
man. His soldierly qualities are to be transferred to a Christian soil. But if you want
to do that, you must approach Cornelius *as*
a soldier. You must allow Christianity to
come to him in a military form. If you look
at the narrative in this light you will see
how singularly appropriate the experience was

to the man. Consider for one thing that the entire constitution of an army rests on mutual dependence. No one can be a successful soldier as an individual; he requires the co-operation of his fellows. Imagine that what Cornelius wanted had been, not the spirit of Christ, but the spirit of Mars the god of war On what condition could Mars have promised his spirit to Cornelius? Only on the condition that the same spirit should be shared by many others, and that the common inspiration should make itself felt in the ranks. One soldier can no more make a victory than one swallow can make a summer. If there is a divided interest, there is a divided allegiance. If one part of the ranks has the notion that another part is animated by a different spirit, the former will not only distrust the latter— they will distrust their own strength, will be paralysed in their own energy. If the god of war had appeared to Cornelius he must have told him that the state of things in Cæsarea would be affected by the state of things at Joppa.

Now, to this phase of the soldier-life Christianity made appeal when it spoke to Cornelius. He had asked the spirit of Jesus in room of the spirit of Mars; yet the new spirit addressed him in the garb of the old. God revealed Himself as the leader of an army, and Cornelius was made to feel that he was being treated as a soldier. The voice said to him: 'Get as many as you can to take an interest in the cause in which *you* are interested. Enlist your two servants and the soldier who waits upon you. Enlist your kinsmen and friends. Enlist the sympathies of Simon Peter and those who are in his train. Let the representatives of all classes give a subscription to your cause—the domestic, the soldier, the church-dignitary, the church-worker, the companions of the social hour. Let them each have a stone in the temple, a window in the building. Bring me not your own heart alone, but the sense that other hearts are in union with yours.'

This, then, I take to be the first reason for the protracted process in the conversion of

Cornelius. The design is to transplant a soldier, and therefore he is approached as a military man—as one who has always associated victory with the co-operation of the many. But I come to a second reason for the protraction of the process, and one which also lies in the appeal to a soldier. For, an army is characterised, not only by the mutual dependence of its members, but by their common life of sacrifice. In time of war the essence of military life is its sacrificial character. I say, in time of war. There may be licence in time of peace—the Roman soldier was then no paragon. But in war there is no life so full of sacrifice. Nor do I think that the main stress of military sacrifice lies in the hour of battle. There have been men in the heat of battle who have for a time been unconscious of their wounds. It seems to me that the sorest part of a soldier's military life is in the things which *defer* the battle, in the objects which impose delay. It is in the long and weary marches, in the treading of arduous ground, in the exposure to thirst and hunger,

in the fatigue and lassitude which accompany
a burning sun, in the demand to keep up the
spirit when there is no excitement, no call to
action, no enemy in view—it is there that the
sacrifice of the soldier appears. I believe that
the deepest sacrifices in the soul of man are not
in life's actual battlefield, but in its moments
of silent endurance. Many a man can resist
the winecup in company who cannot resist it in
solitude ; for the idea of a thing is ever more
powerful than itself, and its image in the heart
outweighs its image in the hand. The life of
the soldier has embodied a truth of humanity.

Now, it is to this life of the soldier that in
the case of Cornelius Christianity appeals.
Cornelius is in hot haste to reach his goal—
the Advent of the Divine Spirit. That will be
to him the beginning of the real battle with
sin ; the day of the Spirit's coming will be to
Cornelius the day of conquest—and with all his
might he longs for it. But he must be treated
as a soldier ; he must be made to pass through
a soldier's sacrifice. The conquest might come
at once ; but that would not be the revelation

to a soldier. God must speak to Cornelius in his own language—and that language is military sacrifice. Instead of reaching his goal in a moment, let him wait for it anxious days, march for it long miles, weave for it arduous plans. Let him for the sake of it submit to the temporary loss of two of his servants. Let him for a time dispense with the services of his favourite attendant—a soldier who knows his special wants and when to meet them. Let him, above all, sink his pride. Proud Roman as he was, representative of Roman conquest as he was, let him bow the knee to one who had been a fisherman of Galilee and acknowledge that in matters spiritual the peasant was his liege lord. I think there is something grandly appropriate in the delay imposed on the soldier Cornelius.

But there is, I think, a *third* element in military life which constitutes a ground for the appropriateness of the delay. The life of the soldier, whether he means it or not, is a vicarious one ; it is lived for the sake of others. A man may live sacrificially and yet may live purely for himself. The artist may scorn delights and spend laborious days, yet he may be animated by a motive essentially selfish— the achieving of some work that will perfect his fame. But the average soldier can have no such motive. To a man of the ranks, even to a man, like Cornelius, a little above the ranks, the chance of winning distinction is infinitesimally small; and the pay is not worth striving for. There is an elimination of all personal feeling—even the feeling of enmity. The man is at war with something he does not hate. He is fighting the battle of another—his country. Voluntarily or involuntarily, it is for her he makes long marches, it is for her he bears the drought and the famine, it is for her he endures privation and weariness, it is for her he dares the path of death and braves the mutilation of life and limb. The soldier, whether he knows it or not, whether he accedes to it or not, is working for another's joy.

So, when Christianity comes to Cornelius it appeals to this fact of the military experience. It bids him connect his conversion, not with his own glory, but with the glory of others. It tells him to calculate, not how happy he will be, but how many people he will make happy. And think for a moment how beautifully this purpose is achieved. Cornelius submitted to a process which robbed him of all glory. He took a back seat. He subsided into the place of a passive recipient. He gave the post of action to his servants, to his private attendant, to the Christians at Joppa, above all to Simon Peter. It was to enlarge *Peter*, not to enlarge himself, that Cornelius was directed to the Christian apostle. Cornelius might have reached the kingdom at a bound ; but Peter would have felt sore that a man should mount to heaven without circumcision. The Divine Voice said: 'There must be no soreness on this birthday. I must first *liberalise* Peter—must stoop to win his approval. I must send him up to the roof of the tanner's house at Joppa. I must tell him to look forth upon the sea— that sea on which rested the eyes of my prophet Jonah. And when he remembers Jonah he will remember Nineveh. He will remember how even on the heathen city my compassion failed not to fall—though circumcision was not there, though temple was not there, though rite of Jewish worship was not there. He will remember and he will say, "What God has cleansed let me not call unclean!" And then I shall cry to Peter, "Come thyself, and cure Cornelius!" Cornelius needs him not; but *he* sadly needs Cornelius. He wants to be broadened, deepened, heightened; I shall make him put his hand upon the Gentile and speak peace. For the sake of another's joy Cornelius may well consent to take a lower room.'

Let me now revert to the statement that the design of this picture is to exhibit the transplanting of a soldier—in other words, that it is intended to represent the grafting of military qualities into the Church of Christ. At first sight this is the last kind of transference which could have been thought an object of desire. We can understand very well how the qualities of the domestic servant should be carried over into the many mansions of the Father's house, for the qualities of the domestic servant are, even in the houses of men, Divine virtues— gifts of the grace of God. Obedience to duty, fidelity, honesty, integrity, truthfulness, justice, the absence of self-interest and of eye-service— these are the qualities which mark the good servant in the secular home, and these are the qualities which stamp the good servant in the household of faith. Christianity, as much as life, is a state of dependence; and the form of a servant is required for both. But war— where does *that* find place in the precepts of Christ! Is He not the Prince of Peace! Was not 'Peace' the song over His cradle and the sigh of His last farewell! Were not the makers of peace to be called in a special sense the children of His Father! Where is there room for Cornelius here—for the *soldier* Cornelius! There is room for the *man*; but must he not lay aside his sword and his helmet when he enters the kingdom of Christ! Surely the *red* flowers of man's garden will not be transplanted into the Garden of the Lord!

Yes, they must and they shall. The demand for such transplanting has been loud through all the Christian ages. Why did the Medieval Church initiate orders of sacred knighthood—knights of the temple, knights of St. Mary, knights of St. John? It was because the Medieval Church wanted a section of her sons to be soldiers in spirit and to transfer the qualities of war into the paths of peace. Why has our modern Christianity instituted a Salvation Army? It is because Cornelius is still needed among the Christians—because in peace as well as in war there are wrongs that await redressing. Why does our twentieth century inaugurate in every town a Boys' Brigade? It is because we want Cornelius in the midst of us. It is because we desire that from an early age our youthful generation should learn to associate religion with manliness, to connect the cross of Christ with all that is brave and heroic and noble, and to plant in civil life those very seeds which in the sphere of the warrior made for military glory.

The truth is, what Christian civilisation needs in a time of peace is pre-eminently the presence of Cornelius—the infusion of a military element. We are apt to be ashamed in peace of that which we laud in war. In men on the road to battle we admire abstinence, temperance, caution, care of bodily health, the avoidance of any temptation to any form of physical excess. We count this manly; and why? Because the men are under military orders. But when we see these qualities in time of peace we are apt to call them womanish; and why? Because then the men are *not* supposed to be under military orders, but to be simply timorous, nervous, frightened. Yet, from the Christian point of view, this is a mistake. The man is as truly on the march in peace as in war, and as truly under orders. We want him to *feel* that. We want him to realise that in the common things of life he is on soldier's duty—bound by a tie of honour, pledged by an oath of fealty, dedicated to the service of a government whose rule is over all nations. 'They shall beat their swords into ploughshares and their spears into pruning-hooks' are the words in which is proclaimed the advent of the Prince of Peace. But even in that proclamation there is a tribute paid to the soldier. The old warlike material is not to be thrown away; it is the sword that is to *become* the ploughshare, it is the spear that is to be made the pruning-hook. Cornelius the soldier is not to be annihilated in the resurrection of Cornelius the man. As he ascends in his fiery chariot the military mantle is not to drop from him. It is to be carried into the new kingdom, to be worn in the new world, to be illustrated in the new life. The sacrificial spirit which animates the deeds of war is to be displayed again in the fields of peace.

As he enters the portals of the Christian life Cornelius fades from our view; his form is lost in the crowd, and we see him no more. But though in visible presence he appears not, he reappears in metaphor. Cornelius represents and foreshadows the conquest of Rome by Christ. Viewed in this typical aspect, we do meet him again. Nearly three centuries after, we see his conversion repeated in the conversion by Christianity of the empire itself. There stands Cornelius once more—calling on Peter to help him! There he stands — wielding the military sceptre, but surrendering the sceptre of the heart! There he stands—embodying in converted Rome a union of his own three experiences! His original Paganism is there—heathen rites are baptised into Christian worship. His subsequent Judaism is there—a God is recognised who is holy but hard to be entreated, flawless but far away. His final Christianity is there—the cross has become the watchword of all life and the symbol of all power. And the retention of his soldier-heart is there—with the garment of Christ Rome has put on a fresh military robe. She has increased her fearlessness; she has augmented her fortitude; she has strengthened her power of endurance; she has deepened her determination; she has quickened her loyalty; she has fanned her enthusiasm; she has sharpened her sense of duty; she has almost *created* her spirit of chivalry. The sword has survived in the ploughshare, the spear in the pruning-hook.

LORD, fit me for the ranks of Thine army! Put Thy best robe upon me —the soldier's robe! Give me Thy truly military spirit—the spirit that casteth out fear—love! Fit me for the times of waiting! I am more afraid of the silence than the conflict. Often have I said in the old time, 'If I could get away from the world, I could put off my armour.' Often have I thought, 'If I could leave the scenes of temptation and could rest in some quiet, secluded spot, I might lay aside the soldier's garb.' And lo! when I tried it, I found that I must *add* to my armour. I found that the scene of temptation is not outside of me but within me, that the battlefield is the silent field. I need Thee most, my Father, when I am meeting with myself. I could perform a sacrifice amid the crowd because I feel that the crowd would applaud me for it. But when Thou hast sent the multitude away, when there are no spectators of my struggle, when the flags wave not, the banners stream not, the trumpets blow not, when I am alone in the field with my own will, it is then I need Thine armour, O my God. It is comparatively easy to wrestle after daybreak, for the daybreak distracts me from myself. But *before* the day breaks, I am alone—alone with myself, alone with my erring soul. Arm me, O Lord, arm me for the great battle where there fights but one! Give me a sword for the solitude, a spear for the silence, a helmet for the hermitage, a breastplate for the breathless air! Quicken me for the quiet, fortify me for the fireside, nerve me for the night, strengthen me for the study, warm me for the woodland ramble, inspire me for the inland calm! Let me wear my armour in life's placid hour!

15

Timothy the Disciplined

THERE are some who have professed to read the character by the handwriting. In the case of Timothy we have a task more difficult still; it is to read the character of one man by the handwriting of another. Nearly all we can gather of the inner life of Timothy is wrapped up within two brief letters addressed to him by Paul. They are really a ministerial charge containing practical advices and cautions to Timothy on his appointment to the pastorate of the Church at Ephesus. Are we entitled to take these advices and cautions as indicating Paul's sense of Timothy's weak points? I think we are. When Paul writes a letter it is always a characteristic letter—characteristic, I mean, of the person or persons written to. When he writes to the residents in Rome, he exhibits Christ as 'the power unto salvation'—and why? Because the dweller in that military city was apt to think Christianity a form of weakness. When he writes to the Corinthians, he exhibits Christ as wisdom—and why? Because to the Greek Christianity appeared foolishness. When he writes to the Galatians, he tells them to be not weary in well-doing—and why? Because they had revealed themselves as fickle. When he writes to Philemon, it is to guide him in a personal affair—an affair in which he had temptation to show harshness. Nay, when he writes to Timothy himself on a physical matter, his advice is professedly dictated by a sense of Timothy's infirmity—'Take a little wine for your stomach's sake.' I conclude therefore that, as the physical advice was prompted by Paul's knowledge of a physical weakness, the mental advice was prompted by his knowledge of a mental weakness; and I feel authorised to use these letters as a biographical mirror in which the secrets of the life are revealed and the heart of the man is spread out before us.

Timothy could have started life with the motto, 'Two worlds are mine.' He was born probably at Lystra—a city of Lycaonia. Within him was the blood of two opposite heredities. His mother Eunice and his grandmother Lois were Jewish Christians of the most pious and devoted type. That stream of heredity from the blood of Israel was, however, counteracted by another stream. If his mother was a Jew, his father was a Greek— of what religious persuasion we know not. Timothy was therefore the child of opposite worlds, and it was inevitable that they should strive within him. Israel and Greece were essentially opposed currents. Their difference lay deeper than any religious doctrine; it was constituted by their view of life. The Jew aimed at the repression of nature; the object of the Greek was to give nature full play. The Jew encouraged the sense of obligation; the Greek fostered the thought of spontaneity. The Jew looked upon the universe with awe;

the Greek viewed it as a pleasure-ground. The Jew uncovered his head in the presence of Divine mysteries; the Greek made them subjects of daring speculation. It was evident that the main danger to Timothy lay on the Greek side. Where Judaism embraced Christianity it was sternly Christian; where Greece favoured Christianity its affection was apt to be divided. Probably in the mind of the father Christianity had not passed the stage of a mere favourable recognition. The age of 'many gods' was past; but the age of 'many systems' had taken its place, and the father of Timothy in all likelihood leant towards each in turn. It was not altogether a propitious nest for the maturing of a steady wing.

In the home, however, the mother seems to have had her own way. She brought up the child in the faith of Christ and under the influence of her pious example. He seems to have been early put to active service in the cause of Christianity. When Paul on his missionary journey came to Lystra and first saw him, he was exceedingly young; yet he was already talked of as a helper in the work. Paul was greatly struck with him. He discerned the promise and the potency of a high and useful life which was worth fostering into bloom. He resolved to train him under his own eye. Doubtless he recognised the danger of the counteracting Greek current in his blood and in his home, and thought the removal from his home might modify the action of his blood. Accordingly, he took Timothy with him. He took him as a pupil —one to be trained for higher service. But when next we meet him he is no longer Paul's pupil; he is his companion. He has not indeed entered into the place of partnership vacated by *Barnabas.* It was rather an association of love than of business, and that kind of love which bridges the separation of those divided by a gulf of years. The older man felt himself a protector; the younger clung to his support. Paul realised that he had adopted this youth, become sponsor for him in the eye of heaven. He felt that he was responsible for his eternal welfare—that he had to supply the place which

the good mother had filled and which the in-
different father ought to have filled. A flower
had been committed to him in the Garden of
the Lord; that flower he had to water every
morning and nurture every day.

Was there a possibility that the relation of
Paul and Timothy might ever be reversed—
that Timothy might become the protector and
Paul the recipient? There would have been,
but for one circumstance. It was this—Paul
was never able to realise that Timothy was
growing older. He insisted on always viewing
him as the lad he met in Lystra. On that
occasion Timothy was probably about twenty
years of age. That was an exceedingly young
man to have gained a local reputation among
the Christians; and we could have understood
Paul saying at that time, 'Let no man despise
thy youth.' But he says it some fifteen years
afterwards—when Timothy must have passed
youth's *despicable* stage. The words were
spoken near the end of Paul's life. He had
gone through most of his crisis-moments. He
had been imprisoned in Cæsarea. He had

made his appeal to Cæsar. He had been shipwrecked on his voyage to Rome. He had been acquitted by a Roman tribunal. He had resumed his missionary labours, and, as a final act in them, he had ordained Timothy to the Church of Ephesus. He had returned to Rome. He had been imprisoned once more—in that dungeon from which he was only to issue through the gate of death. It was from that final captivity that he wrote his pastoral counsels to his friend of long years. And it is then most of all that he seems to forget the years. He sees Timothy, not as he is, but as he was. He ignores the fifteen winters whose storms have swept across his brow and whose chills have furrowed his cheek. He sees him in his home at Lystra in all the freshness of life's morning. He sees him between two fires—the fire of devotion to his mother and the fire of admiration for his father. He sees the struggle of his young heart between the Jew and the Greek—between the surrender of will and the specula-tion of intellect. He feels that the same conflict is raging in the world still—nowhere more than at Ephesus, and that the whole current must be breasted by an inexperienced boy. In words which are pathetic in their loss of the sense of time he cries, 'Let no man despise thy youth.'

But have we never seen anything like this *outside* of the New Testament ! Is it not a matter of daily observation ! Do we not know that those who have been the guardians of the young find it very hard to realise their adolescence ! I knew an elderly woman who always spoke of her brothers as 'these boys.' There was not one of them under fifty years of age ; but she had been as a mother to them in youth and she realised not that their youth was gone. It is always the tendency of love to clothe its object with permanence. It is told of St. John that, when an old man, he stood in the streets of Ephesus and cried, 'Little children, love one another!' Probably the 'little children' were nearly as old as himself; but they had been brought up as pupils in his Bible-class and he felt to them as a father. His love was too strong to observe the growing shadow on the dial; it saw the objects of its morning in the same perpetual youth as that in which the Christian saw his Christ—unchanged yesterday and to-day and for ever. Paul, too, had an illusion in the streets of Ephesus; he took a man to be a boy. It was love's cry for permanence. It was the protest of the heart for the continuance of the morning. It was the desire of the spirit that time should write no wrinkle on the azure brow of that sea of life on which he had sailed long years ago.

Timothy, then, stood before the eye of Paul in the garb of a young man. Paul felt that he wanted discipline—that the flower within him must be cultivated. It was not learning he needed; it was pruning. There are men whose temptation comes from their ignorance; the dangers of Timothy came from his knowledge, his culture, his intellectual development. The spirit of Greece was in him, and the spirit of Greece was the spirit of independent thought. Paul dearly loved to think of him as still young; but he felt that his Greek blood made youth a special danger. It was to youth that the seductions of Greece peculiarly appealed. Rome's muscular vigour spoke to manhood; Judea's restraining influence spoke to middle age; but Greece with her morning radiance addressed the spirit of youth and found her most powerful votaries in the children of the spring.

Let me now proceed to indicate some of those weak points of Timothy's youth which Paul by an act of imagination transferred to his riper age. You will find that they will open up to every man a chapter of autobiography and that the weak points of young Timothy are the weak points which are apt to beset the youth of all men. Now, Paul is very emphatic as to the charge which in importance he would place first. It is not the charge which we should expect him to place first. If we were addressing one whom we thought of as a young man and whom we believed to be under special temptation, we should begin by warning him against flagrant sins—against the excesses of the winecup, the excesses of the gaming-table, the excesses of human passion. Paul does not start with any of these; he tells Timothy first and foremost to cherish a reverent spirit towards those in authority! Is not this a strange advice to put in the front ground of a young man's discipline. I do not think so. I think it would be the advice which in actual youth Timothy first needed. What is the root of youth's dangers? It is the resistance to authority. I do not mean the resistance to any particular authority, but to the principle of authority itself. A young man tends to love the fruit because it is forbidden. The fruit in itself is often distasteful to him. Command young Adam to climb the tree of knowledge, and he will probably refuse; forbid him, and that tree will become an object of desire. Youth oftener goes wrong from a false ideal of manliness than from any love of vice. To be free, to be independent, to do what one likes, to reveal the magnificent example of 'I don't care,' to be pointed out as a bold, reckless spirit that fears not the face of man—that is the ideal which swims before the eye of youth and draws it into all perils.

When Paul first met Timothy everything in the young man's blood tempted to the resistance of authority. His youth tempted him, for youth loves to feel itself free. His Greek descent tempted him, for Greece had ever *aspired* to be free. And, strange to say, it must be added that his Christianity itself tempted him. It sounds curious to hear Paul exhort Timothy to pray for kings. We should have thought the charge would be, 'Pray for the poor and destitute.' But we forget that by the early Christian it was the kings, and not the destitute, who were apt to be neglected. The typical primitive Christian looked down upon his temporal rulers. He held that the humble classes were the privileged classes. What he extended to the rich was at most only a patronage. It was not natural that he should pray first for kings. He was a subject of no king but one—the Lord Jesus. The rulers of the world were in possession of a mock dignity — a dignity which belonged, not to them, but to Him. Why should he pray for their wise governing! Was not their government, whether wise or unwise, an obstacle in the march of the King of kings! Had not he a higher allegiance—the allegiance to another world, to a coming world, to a world before whose blaze of glory all the thrones and principalities and powers of earth must wither away! The kings of the nations might take tribute from his hand; they could get no tribute from his soul.

So in all likelihood thought young Timothy in the days when Paul first met him; and Paul transfers his youth to his riper years. He warns him that he is on a quicksand. He tells him to dismiss his contempt for the higher seats of this world. He tells him that, whether they know it or not, the rulers of earth are God's ministers. He tells him that, whether they know it or not, they are responsible for the bearing of a great burden. He tells him that, by reason of this burden, they are objects not for anger but for reverent commiseration— that they have more need to be prayed for than the poor and destitute. He bids him pray for them first of all; he bids him teach his people to pray for them. It is a *new* call to sympathy. Hitherto sympathy has been asked to descend the ladder; it is now asked to go up—to extend its charity to the high places of the earth, to enter into the troubles of those who sit in the upper room.

Let me pass now to a second advice given by Paul to Timothy, or rather to a combination of two advices often supposed to be contradictory. He virtually tells him to avoid two kinds of fast living—the fastness of brain and the fastness of brainlessness. On the one hand he is very anxious that as a pastor he should avoid matters of intellectual speculation. On the other he is equally solicitous that he should not fritter away intellect altogether by living for trivialities and frivolities—'Flee youthful desires!' he says. I have said that these two dangers seem opposite—the one is *over*-thought, the other is thoughtlessness. We think of the former as a slow and quiet life, of the latter as a life of fastness.

The truth is, they are both fast, and may be both equally fast. What do we mean by fastness? Simply that too many sensations are being crowded together in a small space and in a short time. Physically speaking, it matters not what the sensation be. You may be a student living far from the works and ways of men, dwelling in seclusion and solitude, abstaining from the whole round of worldly pleasure, never seen at fancy fête or fashionable ball, and yet you may be living as fast a life as if you were spending your days in a whirl of gaiety. It is the number and the rapidity of your sensations, and not their moral character, that determine the rate at which you are travelling.

Now, it is more than likely that Timothy in his young days was under both of these temptations. Does it seem to us that both could not exist in the same mind—that the one would serve as a counteraction to the other. We forget that this is the very thing which makes their existence in one mind possible. Who, according to the Jewish Scriptures, is the man most taken up with the frivolities of life? Of all people, it is Solomon—the profound student, the deep scholar, the speculative thinker, the man who filled the world with the fame of his wisdom! I used to wonder at the incongruous combination. I see now that it is true to human nature. The typical Solomon is ever the most in danger of becoming frivolous. He needs a reaction. His mind has been on the wing round the stars; it will by and by be on the wing round the candle. He has been revolving the problems of eternity; he will before long revolve in the dance of the hour. It is the very cry for a counteracting influence that drives him from fervour into frivolity.

You will observe where Paul places frivolity; it is in the 'desires.' I do not suppose he was in the least afraid of Timothy's outward morals; I am quite sure he had no cause to be. But Paul did not think this a sufficient ground of safety. If he had been told of Timothy's external purity, he would still have cried, 'Flee youthful desires!' The frivolous man

was to Paul the man who *desired* frivolous
things. The fast man in moral life was he
whose heart was crowded with images of
vanity and with forms of sensual mould. The
contact which Paul feared for Timothy was an
inward contact. He dreaded no company for
a man like the company of his own unre-
generate heart; *there* was his place of temptation, there was his scene of danger. The
frivolities of life were in each man's soul,
and to cherish these in the soul was already
to yield to temptation.

I will mention one other advice of Paul to
Timothy—more directly pastoral than those
preceding, yet dictated like these by the
apostle's memory of the pupil's youth. He
tells him to be a workman 'rightly *dividing*
the word of truth.' The great temptation of
young ministers is to view the word of truth
in a single aspect. Paul says it ought to be
'divided'—given out in portions according to
the needs of the recipient. The youthful
pastor is apt to address perpetually one class.
One such pastor has a philosophic cast;

another is evangelical; a third is purely practical—so we often sum up the special qualities of the preacher. Paul would say that each of the three was in fault through not 'dividing' the word of truth. He would say that one man should combine them all. He will probably have in his congregation representatives of all. The philosopher will be there—studying the mysteries of being. The evangelical will be there—inquiring the way of salvation. The moralist will be there —seeking the path of duty. Paul would say, 'Divide the word of truth—speak to each in turn.' To him the pastoral life is a sacrificial life in which a man ought to put himself in sympathy with the limits of his congregation —to conceive his subject, not as it appears to *him*, but as it must appear to different modes of mind. He must empty himself of his own predilections—must think with the thoughts of others. He must see deeply with the student, simply with the children, practically with the workers and toilers. He must give to each, not his own favourite portion, but the portion to which each is suited. He must not descant on Dives and Lazarus at the bedside of an invalid, nor expound the case of the ten virgins to a penitent seeking rest. He must be appropriate—which literally means, he must give to every one his own. *That* is the right 'dividing' of the word of truth.

Now, Paul may have observed in Timothy's youth a tendency to this one-sidedness. There was everything to favour its existence. The Greek blood within him made for it in one direction; the Jewish blood within him made for it in another. The spirit of youth itself favoured it. Youth is ever apt to be one-sided, and therefore inappropriate. Young people tend to say the thing unsuited to a particular occasion, and they do so simply because they are one-sided. The cure for them, the cure for Timothy, the cure for all of us, is Christianity—the power to stand in the place of another. That is what makes the religion of Christ differ alike from the Gentile and the Jew; it can incorporate itself in the sympathies of both. It can divide a portion of the soul between either combatant, and therefore can beat with the heart of each. The imitation of Christ is the imitation of one who emptied himself, who clothed himself in the likeness of others, who strove to live in the experience of those beneath him. Only in the effort to follow this life can man avoid the partialities of the Gentile and the Jew.

There is one little point to which I should like to direct attention. Did you ever ask yourself why it is that before administering this discipline to Timothy Paul himself assumes such a humble attitude? Instead of opening with a tone of authority, he begins his letter by telling Timothy what a miserable creature he himself had been—a blasphemer, a persecutor, an injurer of men, a man who for his present position was entirely indebted to the mercy of God. And can you fail to see why Paul begins by taking the lowest room? It was in accordance with his own sublime exhortation, ' If a man be overtaken in a fault, restore such a one in the spirit of meekness.'

He means, in other words, 'Do not address him from a lordly height; let him see that you too have tripped in your day.' That is what Paul wanted Timothy to see. He did not wish the pupil to look upon him as a demi-god. He knew that the basis of all teaching is sympathy, and that sympathy demands a common experience. He comes to Timothy, not in his latest robes, but in his original rags. He speaks to him, not from the top of the ladder, but from its base. He pleads with him, not as one who was born to angelic purity and has never breathed the air of evil, but as one who has known corruption, who has felt temptation, who has touched sin, who has learned the pain of struggle, and who even now is unable to ascribe his salvation to any merit of his own. The discipline from such a man has strength, but no sting.

LORD, when I go to discipline my brother-man, let me remember his environment! Let me remember Timothy's youth, and that the passions of youth are strong! Let me remember his Greek blood that cries for novelty in every form—that flies to-day on the wings of fancy, to-morrow on the pinions of pleasure! Let me remember his Pagan influences, and how many voices in the Garden urge him to climb the tree! Let me remember, above all, my own youth, my own heredity, my own first surroundings! When I visit my erring brother, let me put on my garment of yesterday! Let me not go to him wearing that best robe which Thou hast brought forth for me, and displaying that bright ring which claims me as Thy child! Let me fold Thy fair garment and lay it by; let me take off Thy bright ring and put it aside! Bring me the mean attire of my morning! Bring me the squalid garb in which *first* I met Thee! Bring me the tattered rags in which of old I stood before Thy door! I will go to my brother, clothed in the likeness of sinful flesh. I will go to him with ringless hands, with shoeless feet, with prideless gait. I will go to him and say, 'I come to thee from thine own valley—from humiliation kindred to thine. I too have been among the swine. I too have been a child of the famine. I too have been content to feed on the husks for a time. By no merit of mine am I saved; while I was yet afar off my Father saw me. Receive thy hope from *me*, thy comfort from me, thine example from me! Learn from my rags thy possible riches! See in my meanness thy possible majesty! Behold in my lowliness thy possible ladder! Read in my corruption thy possible crown! So, on the stepping-stones of my dead self, may'st thou rise to higher things.'

16

Paul the Illuminated

IN the chapters on Barnabas, Mark, and Timothy I have alluded to many of the outward incidents in the life of Paul. I do not intend to traverse these lines again. I do not intend to traverse *any* historical lines. And for this reason: The difference between Paul and the other figures of the Gallery is not an outward difference. If you look at him merely in the external acts of his life, you will find nothing that marks him out as a man of unique experience. I do not know of any historical fact in Paul's experience which I am not prepared to parallel with the experience of those already considered. Did Paul reject Christ; so, for a moment, did Peter. Did Paul miraculously escape from prison; so also did Peter. Did Paul suffer shipwreck; so, to

an equal extent, did Peter. Did Paul turn a
somersault; so did John. Did Paul write
compositions of the most divers kinds; so did
John. Did Paul receive a vision of heavenly
things; so did John. Was Paul suddenly convinced of the power of Jesus; so was Thomas.
I could multiply parallels almost indefinitely
to show that the outward life of the Gentile
apostle is not essentially distinct from the
lives of his fellow-Christians. What distinguishes Paul is an experience from within—an
illumination from the spirit, the rising of an
inner sun. It is the fact that this man after
conversion did the same kind of work which
he had been doing before, and that yet by an
added light in his soul he found it to be wholly
new. His work as Saul of Tarsus was the
building of a temple; his work as Paul the
Apostle was the building of a temple too.
Yet, what he felt was not uniformity but
difference, contrast, revolution. Outwardly
he was engaged in the old things; but in
the very act he was constrained to cry, 'Old
things are passed away.' Whence came this

paradox? From what he himself calls a shining in the heart. The change was in the region of the spirit. Sun and moon and stars remained the same; mountain, river, and stream abode in their wonted place; but within his soul a new presence had arisen, and by its potency and power every object of his past was transformed and glorified.

The crisis hour of Paul's life was his transition from Judaism into Christianity. What was that transition? We are so familiar with the fact that we are apt to forget what it represents. What is the spiritual difference between the Jew and the Christian? It is easy to state the *doctrinal* difference; but that of the spirit lies deeper. Let me try to exhibit the contrast in the form of a little parable.

A certain father had two boys whom he was very desirous to bring up good. He thought this would best be accomplished by inuring them to a habit of life. Accordingly, he made a proposal to them. He promised to give each of them a penny for every hour of the day in which they should abstain from doing any bad action. As the sleeping hours were inevitably included in such a bargain, it was really an offer to each of two shillings a day for total abstinence from wicked deeds. The elder brother accepted the proposal with alacrity; the younger refused—he preferred his freedom. The elder brother got the name of being virtuous. He did not, indeed, uniformly make his two shillings, for there was always some hour of some day in which he transgressed; but out of each day he always gathered *something*. The younger, on the other hand, was deemed reckless, careless, godless; hardly an hour passed in which he had not his hand in something wrong. The one brother was called the man of God, the other the man of Satan.

But in process of time a thing happened which made one section of the community change its mind. The brothers chanced one day to pass a picture in a shop window—it was that of a man walking through the scenes of a malignant pestilence in the sheer hope of alleviating human pain. The elder brother looked at the picture with indifference. The younger gazed, lifted up his hands and cried, 'I believe in that man; that is the man I should like to serve, should like to follow, should like to imitate.' And the by-stander said: 'It is this *younger* brother that deserves the prize. Incorrect as his life comparatively is, though there is not an hour in which he does not commit faults to which his brother is a stranger, he has yet reached in one thought, in one aspiration, in one admiring look, a height which through all the laborious days that brother has never climbed.'

Now, the elder brother of this parable is the Jew; the younger is the Christian. The former makes the attempt to count his deeds of abstinence. The latter keeps no reckoning of his deeds; but in his room there hangs a picture of surpassing beauty—a picture he has bought and on which he gazes continually; it is the description of an act of love by which a Divine spirit gave his life for the world. The difference between the Jew and the Christian is the difference between the tied hand and the winged mind. It is quite possible that the force of outward law may keep a man all his life from injuring his neighbour; yet such a man will be no nearer to the beauties of holiness than had he been living in a state of open war. But suppose that, instead of tying his hands, you liberated his heart, suppose that, instead of paralysing him with fear, you quickened him with a sense of beauty, suppose that you confronted him, not with the penalties of doing harm, but with a picture of doing good, you would give him in a moment the door of access into a purity which all the years of his mere moral abstinence have failed to reveal to his sight. The picture on which he would look would be beyond his present strength; and he would know it to be so. But none the less it would be the true measure of the man, the prophecy of his coming self, the foreshadowing of that height which he is destined to win.

Let us return for a moment to the parable of the two boys. I have indicated that the bystanders take different sides. Some go with the elder brother who keeps the laborious hours; others adhere to the younger who gazes on the beautiful picture. Now, Paul at first sided with the former class. He thought that the promised sum ought to be given to the boy who made himself a drudge. He was very angry with the seductive picture which had seemed to open up a short and easy way. He was so angry that he could not keep away from it. He wanted to see where its power of seduction lay—to study it that he might refute it. So he went daily to look at the picture, and gazed on it with an adverse eye. But, as he looked, there happened a strange thing—the picture crept into his soul. He had sought to find the secret of its power with the view of refuting it. He did find the secret of its power; but it refuted *him*. The gaze of anger was transmuted into a gaze of rapture. He was conquered by the spectacle of moral purity. He saw a spotless soul walking amid the dread pestilence of sin—treading the infected streets, touching the unclean garments, breathing the deadly vapours, nursing the stricken patients, haunting the scenes of horror from which the world had fled, and at last sinking exhausted by the wayside and purchasing the life of others by the sacrifice of his own. All this Paul saw, and for the first time there woke within him a sense of what sin really was, what purity really was, what the service of God really was. In one instant he rose far above all the steps he had been climbing for years. By one thought, by one vision, by one sight of an ideal man, he reached a height which a thousand acts had failed to win. He said: 'I believe in that man—he expresses all that I should like to be. Will not this be God's measure of me, God's estimate of me, the standard of judgment by which God will see my capacities for good! Will He not test me for the time to come, not by what I am, but by what I wish to be!'

This was the moment of Paul's illumination. It was the moment in which there entered into his soul the one love of his life—the only

passion which ever stirred his heart. Christ
has appealed to men in many ways—sometimes in fear, sometimes in reverence, sometimes in speculation, sometimes in the sense
of protection. To Paul He is exclusively an
object of love. Every other phase of thought
is absorbed in that *one*. He tells us so
himself. In that magnificent hymn of his
which will live as long as the Christian ages,
he sings not only the everlastingness but the
predominance of love. He sings how in his
own experience all virtues have *melted* into
love—how faith has faded into its certainty,
how prophecy has died in its fulfilment, how
knowledge has yielded to its light. The inward history of Paul is the history of his love
—the history of that process by which love
filled all things.[1] This, from an artistic point
of view, is the real interest of the apostle's
life. His missionary journeys interest the
evangelist, his doctrinal system attracts the

---

[1] Love came to Paul as self-enlightenment, to John as self-
surrender ; Paul never needed self-surrender—at no time did
he live for himself.

theologian; but what distinguishes him to the eye of the artist is that gradual process of illumination through which, step by step and sphere by sphere, every part of the universe was lit up, until the world became to him 'the fulness of Him that filleth all in all.'

I have spoken of Paul's illumination as a gradual process. I should like to explain what I mean by this. I do not think that after his conversion Paul ever changed his mind on a matter of doctrine—his faith in Christ was as strong at the beginning as it was at the end. Nor do I think that Paul's actual love for Christ went through any modification; it began perhaps unconsciously, and was revealed to himself suddenly, but from that time I think it never varied. When I speak, however, of a gradual process in Paul, I mean, not an enlargement of his love, but an enlargement of its sphere. These two things are quite distinct. A child's love for his father may be perfect without being perfectly illuminating. It may be an isolated and isolating love—may keep him from seeing the beauty and acknowledging the real attractions of the other persons around him. Illumination is not the heating but the lighting process. Paul's love to Christ was as perfect when he wrote to the Thessalonians as when he penned his letters to Timothy; but it was less far-seeing, or, to speak more accurately, it shed less light upon surrounding things. The triumph of love is not the amount of its passion; it is the number of things which it irradiates. The development of Paul is not a deepening of conviction, not a progress in doctrine, not an intensifying of emotion, not a growth in the spirit of sacrifice; it is an enlargement of the sphere of love. He says himself that his Christ was destined to fill all things within his universe. And so He was; but the process was not an instantaneous one. Paul did not at once see all things subject to Him. At first his Christ seemed to dwell apart from the world and to be sharply divided from the world. Step by step the barriers were broken down, and, as each barrier fell, the light ran over. Field was added to field where the Divine Presence could walk in the cool of the day, till, in the fulness of Paul's experience, the world on every side was 'bound by gold chains about the feet of God.'

What is the common process of love's enlargement? Take a human love; take what we generally term romantic love. What are the stages through which it is wont to pass? I think there are four. At first it is a hope—something to be realised to-morrow. Then it is a present possession, but reserved as yet only for garden hours when we are free from the bustle of the crowd. By and by its range is widened—it becomes a stimulus for the great duties of life; it comes out from the garden into the city; it nerves to do and to bear. At last it reaches its climax—it comes down to trifles. It glorifies the commonplace; it finds sermons in stones and sonnets in the dust. Little things are magnified; unromantic things are glorified. We do prosaic work. We perform menial duties. We go through cheerful drudgery. We pluck thorns instead of flowers, and smile at the pain. The latest stage of love's enlargement is when it touches the things on the ground.

And this is the order in the enlargement of *Paul's* love. How do we know this? Because we have in our possession a copy of his love-letters. They form a series stretching over some fifteen or sixteen years. If we cannot always point to their exact date, we can tell at least the order in which they come. And as we study them in this light we make a discovery. We find that the series is a series of milestones. The letters of Paul are a progressive history. They describe the onward march of his love—and none the less effectively because they do it unconsciously. You may not trace landmarks in his *theology*. As you travel from the Thessalonians to the Corinthians, from the Corinthians to the Ephesians, from the Ephesians to the Pastorals, you may not be able to point to a spot in which a new doctrine has taken the place of the old. But there is one thing you can see—the bird is flying over a larger field. The bird is love. Its wings have not increased in strength, its plumage is not more beautiful, its flight is not more high; but its range is wider over the earthly plain. The history of love's enlargement in Paul is identical with the history of its enlargement in you. He reaches the goal of freedom by the same road. There are no two kinds of love where love is pure. Paul's devotion to his Christ was not different in essence from your devotion to an earthly friend ; and the enlargement of his devotion to his Christ followed the same steps which enlarge the compass of your human devotion. Christ is to him first the object who is coming, then the object that is already in the *soul*, then the object that gives strength for the *world*, and lastly the object which has glorified the things once deemed insignificant and trivial. Let us glance at each of these.

When Paul's love for Christ first rose, it rose as a hope. Like romantic love, it presented itself as the prospect of to-morrow. Christ was coming—He would change all things, would beautify all things. This present system did not represent Him; but this present system was ready to vanish away. 'It is not here,' he cries to the Thessalonians, 'that you can expect to see Christ's glory; His glory can only appear in the *transformation* of the world. He is coming to transform, to purify, to brighten. It is true, some of you are expecting Him too soon. The world has not yet thoroughly revealed its badness; it is kept in check by the laws of the Roman empire. But the time is coming when that empire shall be crushed and broken; then the passions of men shall be loosed and you will learn your need of God's morning. Your hope is in the future; your sun is in to-morrow's sky; your dawn is in the coming day.'

Remember, the Christ whom Paul first saw was the Christ in heaven. He never gazed upon the man of Galilee. His earliest vision was the vision of a Jesus glorified. Not on

the road to the cross did Christ meet him;
He came to him panoplied in heavenly
splendour. What his inner eye beheld was
the Christ of the future—a Christ of majesty,
a Christ of power, a Christ who came clothed
in the lightning and wreathed in the con-
queror's robe. That was the first Christian
image in Paul's soul. Is it wonderful that it
should have been the first Christian image in
his writings! Is it wonderful that his earliest
note of missionary music should be 'Jesus
and the Resurrection'! Is it wonderful that
at first his love should look forward instead
of either back or around — should begin,
neither with memory nor with fruition, but
with an act of hope! The being whom he
loved had come to him as a prospect, not
as a possession. He had flashed before him
as an object to strive for, as a prize which
to-morrow was to win; and therefore within
the folds of to-morrow lay all his salvation
and all his desire.

But a second stage was coming; you will
find it in the transition from Athens to

Corinth. Up to the time when he reached the summit of Mars Hill he had preached Christ and the Resurrection — the Christ behind the veil. But after his descent from Mars Hill his love found a new sphere. He began to think, not of the Christ in the heavens, but of the Christ in the soul. There broke upon him the conviction that even in this world there might be a little green spot where he could meet with Jesus. There was a garden plot on earth which was not *of* earth — the region of the human spirit. Thither he might retire betimes and be at peace. Within the scene of turmoil there might be a moment of supreme joy, a place of placid rest, a bower in whose sweet retirement the burden and the heat might be forgotten and where the soul could revel in communion with the object of its love.

Here, then, Paul's love has reached a higher stage of illumination; it has found a place within the present world. But the world itself to the eye of Paul has not yet been illuminated — it only contains a spot where illumination is *possible*. That spot is thoroughly fenced in ; the common round of life enters not within its precincts. What is Paul's attitude towards the world at this time ? It has been described as an adverse one. I would define it rather as one of indifference. He is in that stage of love in which everything is ignored but the garden — the place of meeting with its object. His language towards the outside is not that of enmity but simply of uninterestedness. He does not condemn marriage ; he says it is a matter of no consequence whether one is married or single. He does not condemn merchandise ; he says that buying and selling are things of no religious moment. He does not condemn the use of life's good things ; he says that he has entered into a joy which to him personally would make the using of them or the refraining from them a question of absolute unimportance—these things have lost their glory by reason of an all-excelling glory. A young woman of my acquaintance asked a revival preacher if he thought there was any harm in dancing; the answer was, 'I do not see how you can find time.' I think that at this period such would have been Paul's reply to any one asking whether in the light of Christ he was entitled to take part in worldly pleasures; he would have said, 'The time is short.' To his mind it was not so much that Christ opposed anything as that He dwarfed *everything*. He eclipsed to Paul even the glories of nature. Men have wondered at his silence on physical beauty; some have explained it by the theory that the thorn in his flesh was blindness. It may have been. But, to account for Paul's silence about physical beauty, we need no thorn. It came from his flower. There was a presence in the air which to him put out sun and moon and star. It struck him blind, not by darkness, but by light. It dimmed the skies by its glory. It withered the flowers by its radiance. It lowered the mountains by its majesty. It supplanted eye and ear, and reigned in their stead. The world's beauty to Paul was crucified in Jesus.

I come to the third stage in the illumination of Paul's love. Its birthplace was Cæsarea and within the walls of a prison.[1] Strange that a prison should have been the scene of Paul's enlargement! Yet, paradoxical as it seems, it was in prison that the world expanded to his view. Here, for the first time, he saw Christianity through a telescope; and things which he had deemed so far off as to be outside the pale of Christ were brought so nigh as to be recognised as parts of His kingdom. Christ had already been recognised by Paul as the head of the Church; but in that prison at Cæsarea He became more—the head of the state, the head of all states. Within the walls of that prison the Christian world burst the boundaries Paul had assigned to it. The secular became sacred in its greater manifestations—its appearance through the telescope. Hitherto in the apostle's mind the kingdom of Christ had been limited to the sitters at

---

[1] I have here followed the view of Meyer that the Epistles to the Ephesians and the Colossians belong to the Cæsarean rather than to the Roman Captivity—though, unlike him, I assign to Rome Philippians and Philemon.

the communion table. But here, as if by an opening in the heavens, there was revealed a wider empire of the Son of Man. He was no longer merely the king of saints ; He was the king of kings—the head of principalities and powers. The Church was no more a little garden walled in from the outside world ; the outside world was itself the vestibule into the Church. All kingdoms were Christ's kingdom ; all history was Church-history ; all events among the nations were events in the sphere of religion. Paul began to see his Christ outside the limits of Eden and apart from the trees of the Garden. He had traced His hand in the breaking of communion bread; he began to trace it in the powers called natural —in the field of politics, in the field of war, in the field of literature, in the field of human eloquence. There dawned upon him the conviction that salvation might enter the soul by a secular door. If Christ was the head of the state, if the state as well as the Church was His embodiment, then, in the service of the state, a man might well feel that he was performing mission labour. The politician in the very pursuit of his politics, the senator in the very exercise of his art, the soldier in the very act of defending his country, might claim to be evangelists. In the light of such a thought as that, Paul might well realise that his own profession was taken by violence, and that the secular heroes of every age could claim him as a brother.

Such was the illumination of Paul's love in the sphere of the telescope. But what of its illumination in the sphere of the microscope. He had seen the sacredness of the state with its mighty principalities and powers. But there was an opposite to the state and its principalities — the home and its commonplaces. This is the last stage in the progress of romantic love. It reaches every spot before that. It begins with the future; then it finds in the present a secret place where the world cannot come ; then it wreathes itself round the *great* things of the world. All these Paul had passed through. But the final stage remained—love's illumination of those things of

the world which were *not* great—the gilding
of the commonplaces of home. That also
was coming. Already in the latest sections
of what I consider the Cæsarean Epistles we
find traces of the idealising of home; yet it
does not there get the first place. It is in
Paul's last missionary journey that there
strikes the final hour of his spiritual pilgrim-
age. There, in his epistle to Titus, his love
reaches its final glory by reaching the ground.
There, for the first time, the subject from
beginning to end is the secular home-life of
the Christian congregation. To the eye of
youthful romance it is a most wingless letter.
There are no flights in the air, no speculations
about futurity, no expositions of Christian
doctrine. Their place is taken by home precepts—precepts for the hearth, precepts for the
household, precepts for the unity of the family
bond. Each generation is addressed in turn—
the grandfather and grandmother, the son and
daughter, the children of the son and the children of the daughter; while even their relation
to the domestic servants is not forgotten. Yet,

wingless as the letter seems, it is really a proof that love's wings are perfected. In the illumination of home's prosaic duties the spirit of romance has reached its utmost stretch of pinion. Its climax is not the mount but the vale; its glory is not the diamond but the dust. When Paul's love had illuminated the commonplaces of home, it might well break into the cry, ' I have fought a good fight, I have finished my course; henceforth there is laid up for me a crown of glory.'

L ORD, illuminate this world to me! Often have I asked Thine illumination of the spheres beyond; it seemed a harder thing to light up heaven than to light up earth. But I have found that I was wrong. It is for humble things I most need Thy revealing. It is easy for me to worship in the solemn hour of night when the pulse of life is silent and the world's tread beats low. It is easy for me to worship when the sacred symbols are in my hand and the sacred memories are in my soul. But the clouds and darkness that are round about Thee lie not in heaven's mysteries; they lie in earth's shallows. It is bewildering to see Cana anxious only about a deficiency in the feast when the real problem is one of life and death; it makes me say, 'Religion is unreal.' Yet Thou hast stooped to the shallows of Cana, Thou hast thrown Thyself into sympathy with the wants of children. I can find Thee, I can find Thy cross, even in the land of trifles. Help me, when there, to seek that cross! Help me to repeat Thy sympathy with Cana! Help me to wade in the shallows with the child! Help me to remember needs that I have surmounted, to respect desires that I have outgrown! Help me to go down to the things I *used* to wish for — to recall the claims of yesterday! Then shall I be fervent even amid frivolities, true even amid trifles, Christian even amid crudities. Then shall I find pearls in the pool, gold in the grass, sapphires in the snow, treasures in the trodden way. Then shall Thy cross be planted in its most unlikely soil—the place of worldly pleasure, the ground which the trivial tread. Love will have lighted her final torch when she has illuminated the wants of Cana.

OTHER BIBLE CHARACTER STUDIES

**George Matheson: "Portraits of Bible Characters"
series** (Foreword by Warren W. Wiersbe)

Are your looking for fresh insights into Bible characters
that will uplift and challenge your spiritual growth? Then
this series will meet that need. The moral insights and
spiritual beauty of these short studies are remarkable and
refreshing.

Warren W. Wiersbe says of this blind author, ". . . in my
opinion, no evangelical writer, including the great Alexander Whyte, surpasses George Matheson in this whole
area of Bible biography. "The Portraits of Bible Characters"
series combine theological truths with poetic insights to
form unique, fascinating portraits.

PORTRAITS OF BIBLE MEN — First Series
Adam, Abel, Enoch, Noah, Abraham, Isaac, Jacob, Joseph,
Moses, Joshua, Samuel, David, Solomon, Elijah, Elisha, Job

PORTRAITS OF BIBLE MEN — Second Series
Ishmael, Lot, Melchizedek, Balaam, Aaron, Caleb, Boaz,
Gideon, Jonathan,Mephibosheth, Jonah, Hezekiah, Isaiah,
Jeremiah, Ezekiel, Daniel

PORTRAITS OF BIBLE MEN — Third Series
John the Baptist, John, Nathanael, Peter, Nicodemus, Thomas, Philip, Matthew, Zacchaeus, James, Barnabas, Mark, Cornelius, Timothy, Paul

PORTRAITS OF BIBLE WOMEN
Eve, Sarah, Rebekah, Rachel, Miriam, Deborah, Ruth, Hannah, Mary the mother of Christ, Mary, Mary Magdalene

Ivor Powell: "Bible Characters" series
The author, in his gifted manner, presents short studies and unique outline sketches of Bible characters in a most vivid and attractive style.

BIBLE CAMEOS
These eighty graphic "thumb nail" sketches are brief biographies of Bible people. Pungent and thought-provoking studies.

BIBLE HIGHWAYS
Scripture texts are linked together as a chain suggesting broad *highways* through the entire Bible as one travels in thought through the lives and incidents of Bible characters and topics.

BIBLE PINNACLES
A spiritual adventure into the lives and miracles of Bible characters and the meaningful parables of our Lord.

BIBLE TREASURES
In refreshingly different style and presentation, eighty Bible characters are vividly portrayed.

Frances VanderVelde: WOMEN OF THE BIBLE

With a rare combination of biblical knowledge, historical background and human warmth, Frances VanderVelde provides a memorable collection of studies about thirty-one Bible women. Adhering strictly to factual accounts in the Scriptures, the author, using imagination and insights, pictures each Bible character as contemporary. Women as diverse as Queen Esther, the Samaritan at the well, Sarah, Herodius and Priscilla have a message, whether negative or positive, for today's women.

The practical applications drawn from each woman's life make this a unique tool for study. Adaptable for individual or group use, this superlative book offers suggestions for discussion at the end of each chapter. Relive the lives of the following Bible women:

Eve, Sarah, Lot's wife, Hagar, Rebekah, Rachel, Leah, Dinah, Jochebed, Miriam, Rahab, Deborah, Naomi, Hannah, Esther, Mary, the mother of Christ, Elizabeth, Anna, Martha, Mary of Bethany, Herodius and her daughter, the Syro-Phoenician woman, Salome, the Samaritan woman, Mary Magdalene, Sapphira, Dorcas, Lydia, Priscilla, and Lois and Eunice.